Express Cooking

Express Cooking

Make Healthy Meals Fast in Today's

Quiet, Safe Pressure Cookers

Barry
Bluestein
and
Kevin
Morrissey

HPBooks

HPBooks
Published by The Berkley Publishing Group
A division of Penguin Putnam Inc.
375 Hudson Street
New York, New York 10014

First edition: January 2000

Published simultaneously in Canada.

The Penguin Putnam Inc. World Wide Web site address is
http://www.penguinputnam.com

Library of Congress Cataloging-in-Publication Data

Bluestein, Barry.
    Express cooking : make healthy meals fast in today's
quiet, safe pressure cookers / by Barry Bluestein and
Kevin Morrissey.
        p.   cm.
    Includes index.
    ISBN 1-55788-326-2
    1. Pressure cookery.   2. Quick and easy cookery.
I.   Morrissey, Kevin.   II. Title.

TX840.P7   B58   2000
641.5'87—dc21
                                                    99-047353
                                                       CIP

Printed in the United States of America

10 9 8 7 6 5 4 3 2 1

For Jill Van Cleave, the inspiration for this book
and a constant source of encouragement, erudition,
humor, warmth, and goodwill.

Acknowledgments

We're grateful to John Duff, Jeanette Egan, Kristen Green, Barbara O'Shea, and all the other talented folks at Penguin Putnam Inc. who graciously lent their time and talent to make this book a success.

For providing products for us to pressure-cook with, we thank Mark Sterwald at the Mirro Co., Melanie Northfield at Fagor, Vivian Broeski at Magefesa, Robin McKenzie at Kuhn Rikon, Joann O'Gara at Presto, Joya Ricci at Salton Housewares, and Richard Braun at Zand and Associates, representing T-Fal. Special thanks to Barbara Garrett, Eric Endres, and Duane Smith at Windmere on behalf of Meal 'N Minutes.

Last, but never least, a tip of the toque to the many friends and colleagues who support our effort daily—including Dana Benigno, Nicole Bergere, Tammy Blake, Ann Bloomstrand, Chris Broyles, Lizanne Ceconi, Lisa Ekus, Ken Grispin, Deborah and Jim Hendricks, Betty Kennedy, Grant Kessler, Merrilyn Lewis, Claudia Clark Potter, Leslie Revsin, David Saffer, Martha Schueneman, and Beth Shepard.

Contents

Introduction

Lots of people have opinions about pressure cookers, few if any of which are neutral. We hardly claim to be impartial—it has become one of our goals in life to convince as many cooks as possible just how indispensable the new generation of foolproof pressure cookers are to the way we eat at the start of the twenty-first century.

Those folks whose familiarity with the pressure cooker is limited solely to family legend often cringe at the recollection of apocryphal explosions that left the ceiling coated with culinary debris. Others, lucky enough to have been exposed to modern pressure cooking, know better. In Europe, which led the way in the development of today's safe, silent, and sleek stainless-steel cookers, they are relied on for the preparation of flavorful, nutritious meals at the end of busy workdays. (In industrious Switzerland, for example, the average household owns three.) With the introduction by American manufacturers of electric models that you simply program and walk away from (these are definitely not what grandma used to use), the pressure cooker may now take its rightful place at the forefront of all the time-saving devices that populate our kitchens.

We admit to having felt just a bit nervous when we began this book. Colleagues had convinced us of the many merits of pressure cooking, but our first experiments with an old shake, rattle, and roll jiggle-top model conjured up all those old tales of woe. We've since graduated to the new generation of manual cookers that purr their way through preparation, and we were among the first cooks in the United States lucky enough to try out prototypes of the electric models, which can do just about everything but your taxes automatically. Needless to belabor, we now use one or another of our pressure cookers constantly and for just about everything.

What the Pressure Cooker Is and What It Does Well (Hint: Most Things)

The pressure within a sealed cooker is increased to up to about 15 pounds greater than the normal pressure at sea level, raising the boiling point of water from 212F (100C) to 250F (120C). This enables foods to be cooked in about a third of the normal time, while softening tough fibers and keeping nutrients intact.

In addition to its health benefits in preventing the escape of vitamins and minerals often lost through other cooking methods, the pressure cooker is a natural for reduced-fat cooking. It produces some of the leanest yields of such typically fatty meats as corned beef and duck that we've ever eaten. Nor does pressure cooking require the superfluous addition of oil or butter. We often skip the initial browning steps of traditional recipes, with no apparent ill effects. (This saves time as well. Why, after all, use a time-saving cooker and then waste time with unnecessary browning?) The pressure cooker also readily lends itself to day-ahead cooking; fattier dishes can thus be refrigerated overnight and the fat skimmed off before reheating.

The pressure cooker is best known for speeding up preparation of grains and legumes of all sorts (normally long-cooking beans cook not only in a fraction of the time but with a homogeneity of texture all but impossible to achieve when cooked by other means) and for hastening and tenderizing inexpensive cuts of meat, from beef shanks to lamb stew, veal breast to pork butt.

Not only will the pressure cooker work its wonders on many a bargain cut of meat, it will improve the taste and texture of a wide range of other foods, including quick-cooking fish and seafood you might not associate with pressure cooking. Salmon steaks, which are often dry, for example, emerge wonderfully moist. It also yields perfect risotto, without the incremental addition of liquid and frequent stirring; just about the richest stocks you have tasted; and gloriously vibrant and flavorful vegetables, including artichokes whose cooking liquid is far more robust than any dipping sauce you could serve on the side.

We also use the pressure cooker to produce some killer desserts, Barry's favorite quick roast beef supper, succulent whole chickens, and a turkey breast suitable for Thanksgiving dinner. Come to think of it, just about the only things we haven't taken to cooking in the pressure cooker are plain white rice (why bother?) and skinless, boneless chicken breasts (because they taste a bit rubbery to us).

Jiggle-Top Cookers: Most people are familiar with the old-fashioned jiggle-top cookers made by Wearever and Presto. They work perfectly well, albeit somewhat noisily, with a few caveats. Because the jiggle-top cooker does not have a built-in disk on the bottom that allows for internal expansion of the bottom of the pot, it can't be used on flat, smooth-top cooking surfaces. Because steam escapes when the weight jiggles, you will lose some volume of liquid in the pot, so you may need to add extra water, according to the manufacturer's recommendations, when using one of these models, and your yield on stocks and soups may be a bit diminished.

Fixed-Weight Cookers: Fixed-weight cookers are second-generation models and include those made by Fagor in Spain, T-Fal in France, and Presto in the United States. Most models are sturdy, one-piece pots made of rust-resistant stainless steel for easy cleaning, with built-in disks that allow for their use on smooth cooktops. Some steam still escapes through the top, but considerably less in volume and more quietly than with the jiggle-tops. T-Fal has recently introduced a cooker with a window, which allows you to make visual checks on the food's progress.

Spring-Valve Cookers: Including cookers made by Kuhn-Rikon from Switzerland, Fagor, Magefesa from Spain, and Cuisinart (now, unfortunately, out of production), the stainless-steel spring-valve cookers have all the advantages of the fixed-weight models, along with minimal loss of steam (stock yields may actually exceed the volume of water you start with).

Electric Cookers: New electric cookers are now available from Revere Electronics and from Maxim. For starters, they don't require you to

Different Types of Pressure Cookers

turn on your stove, and they operate almost silently, with as minimal a loss of steam as spring-valve cookers. They reach and maintain pressure automatically, and some models can even be programmed to turn on automatically at a desired hour. The only disadvantages we can see in these early models are their somewhat limited capacity (4 to 5 quarts, whereas most manual models hold at least 6 quarts) and the fact that some models operate only at high pressure. When possible, we have given conversions for recipes that we would normally cook at low pressure.

Sizes and Shapes of Cookers

Manual pressure cookers are available in a variety of sizes and shapes, including 4-quart, 6-quart, and 8-quart models. We used 6-quart cookers most of the time in developing the recipes for this book. The 4- and 5-quart models, like the electric cookers, will be a bit too small to hold the likes of whole chickens and ducks or a turkey breast. An 8-quart cooker will work particularly well if you want to feed a crowd—increasing the quantity of ingredients placed in the cooker will not change the cooking time. We also found that this especially tall model was the only one that would accommodate the traditional cylindrical Christmas mold in which we like to steam holiday puddings. Kuhn-Rikon makes a skillet-shaped cooker that works well with anything flat that requires minimal liquid, such as a veal breast or many vegetable dishes.

Safety Features

There was a grain of truth in those stories about pressure cookers blowing their tops in your grandmother's day. They were designed so that if too much pressure built up, the steam valve would blow out to allow steam to escape. Today's models have multiple devices to emit steam and will eventually just release it all with the lid still quite intact. You really shouldn't leave the manual models unattended for great lengths of time; but if you do, the damage will probably be less than if you had let something overcook in a conventional skillet or in the oven. In addition, the modern cookers will not come to pressure if not securely locked, nor can they be opened until the pressure has completely lowered.

Filling the Pressure Cooker: Follow specific recipe directions for the volume of food and liquid to be added to your cooker. Place the food on a trivet (one comes with many models) or on a small wire rack if the recipe calls for elevating the food slightly off the bottom of the pot. As a general guideline, don't fill the cooker more than two-thirds full (one-half full in the case of legumes and grains, which foam quite a bit) and be sure to use at least $\frac{1}{2}$ cup of liquid, or the minimum volume recommended by your cooker's manufacturer.

Bringing Manual Cookers to Desired Pressure: Always make sure the cover is locked in place securely according to the manufacturer's directions before adjusting the setting to the desired pressure. Place the cooker on a burner no larger than the bottom of the pot, and adjust the flame on a gas stove so that it is contained beneath the pot and doesn't shoot up the sides. The majority of our recipes, including those for most soups, stews, meats, vegetables, and grains, call for cooking at high pressure (about 15 pounds). We use low pressure (5 to 8 pounds, according to model) for many poultry preparations, as well as for dishes that have especially thick sauces and for anything that could scorch easily. Some cookers have a middle setting or two, with which you may wish to experiment as you fine-tune your pressure cooking skills. Take care to temper the heat when a recipe calls for bringing the cooker to pressure over other than high heat. You will know pressure is reached in a jiggle-top cooker when the top weight starts jiggling rapidly and continuously, in most fixed-weight cookers when the button depressed in a well on the lid rises flush with the top, and in a spring-valve cooker when the stem in the center of the top rises to show the desired ring.

Maintaining Pressure in Manual Cookers: In most cases, you will need to lower the heat to stabilize pressure once it is reached. If the heat is still too high, steam will automatically be released, causing even the quietest of cookers to sputter and hiss a bit. You will know that the heat has fallen too low on a jiggle-top cooker if it jiggles less than three to four times a minute, on a fixed-weight cooker if the button falls back into its well, and on a spring-valve cooker if the stem falls so that you can no longer see the desired ring. Pressure is maintained automatically in electric cookers.

Pressure Cooking on an Electric Stovetop: Remember that most electric burners will respond more slowly than will gas when you lower the heat to stabilize pressure. Try transferring the cooker from the burner set on high heat to one that has been preheated at a lower setting, or try removing the cooker from the burner briefly to allow the burner to cool down a bit. Do not attempt to use a jiggle-top cooker without a flat bottom disk on a smooth-top cooking surface.

Cooking Times: Cooking times in our recipes begin when the cooker reaches desired pressure. When using a pressure cooker at altitudes of more than 2,000 feet above sea level, you should generally increase cooking times by about 5 percent for every additional 1,000 feet. If you find something not sufficiently cooked when you open the cooker, relock, bring back to pressure, and cook for 1 or 2 minutes more. Most of your favorite stovetop and oven-baked recipes cooked with liquid can be done in a pressure cooker in about one-third the normal cooking time; for conversion tips, see pages 9 to 14.

Releasing Pressure Naturally: The pressure will be released naturally from all types of cookers once they have turned off or been removed from the heat source. This slow method is often preferred with meats that might otherwise toughen and with very liquid contents, such as stocks, which could spurt out were the pressure quickly released. Don't lower the pressure by a quick-release method when natural release is called for—the fact that the food will continue to cook during this longer release process has been factored into the recipe.

Quick-Release by Button or Lever: There are two quick-release methods of lowering pressure. Fixed-weight and spring-valve cookers have a button or lever and electric cookers have a button that can be depressed to release a steady stream of steam, thus reducing the pressure quickly. This is the preferred method for vegetables and other foods that could easily overcook, for delicate desserts that could fall apart if the cooker were moved too precipitously, and for those times when the contents of the cooker are too heavy or cumbersome for it to be moved easily.

Cold Water–Release: The pressure can also be quick-released from jiggle-top, fixed-weight, and spring-valve cookers by carefully transferring the cooker from the cooktop to the sink and running cold water around the top (avoiding the steam valve). This will cause the pressure to drop quickly enough that you will actually hear the locking mechanism release, as it will in all types of cookers once the pressure has lowered. Cold water–release is important to use when cooking grains and legumes that need to stop cooking as soon as done but that produce foam that could bubble up through the valve if you were to release the steam by using the quick-release button or lever.

Opening the Pressure Cooker: Always tilt the lid away from you when opening it, so that any steam or hot water trapped beneath will be directed away from you.

Cleaning and Maintenance: Clean your pressure cooker according to manufacturer's directions; in most cases, warm, soapy water will be sufficient. Before each use, make sure that the steam valve is clear and clean and that the rubber gasket, which may need to be replaced after a few years, is clean and supple. Leave the cover off so that the cooker can air out between uses.

Guidelines for Adapting Your Favorite Recipes to the Pressure Cooker

Anything that is long cooked in a covered dish or pot is a good candidate for adaptation to the pressure cooker, including dishes that are stewed, braised, poached, steamed, boiled, and in many cases baked. You will not be able to convert recipes that call for grilling or broiling or any roasting recipes in which crispness is a desired result.

Determine the estimated cooking time for the various ingredients in the recipe by consulting the charts that follow and those for pressure cooking beans (page 161), grains (page 144), and vegetables (page 124). Use the cooking time and the desired pressure for the longest-cooking ingredient. A chicken breast and long-grain white rice casserole, for example, would be cooked at low pressure for 11 to 12 minutes, the cooking time and desired pressure for chicken breasts.

When combining delicate, quick-cooking ingredients such as seafood or vegetables with other longer-cooking ingredients or sauces, partially cook the longer-cooking items, lower the pressure by a quick-release method, add the seafood or vegetables, bring the cooker back to pressure, and finish cooking the dish. When adapting recipes that contain heavily foaming ingredients such as beans and grains, do not fill the pressure cooker more than about halfway.

Most foods can be cooked at high pressure. Consult the charts to identify the exceptions that we recommend cooking at low pressure if you have a model that has multiple pressure settings. If not, you can cook at high pressure in most cases; reduce the cooking time by about 25 percent. Do not cook dishes with very thick sauces that could easily burn at high pressure.

When cubing or slicing an ingredient, cut all pieces into approximately the same size to facilitate even cooking. If one ingredient is longer cooking than another, cut it into smaller pieces than you do the quicker-cooking ingredients.

The amount of liquid required for pressure cooking will be much less than that needed to cook the same dish by a conventional method on the stovetop or in the oven. Reduce the total volume of liquid (water, wine, stock, juice, or sauce) to the minimum volume for your cooker as noted in the manufacturer's directions. Remember to take all liquid into consideration; for example, a 14½-ounce can of diced tomatoes contains ⅓ to ½ cup liquid along with the tomatoes.

Consult the charts to determine whether it is preferable to let the pressure drop naturally or to lower it by a quick-release method. Let the cooker's pressure drop naturally for very liquid contents, such as stocks and full pots of soup, in which quick-release could send a geyser of liquid spurting up through the steam valve. Natural release is also the preferred method to keep beef and pork dishes tender and to keep delicate desserts intact. For grains and beans, the cold water–release method is the desirable mode of quick-release in a manual cooker.

If you think a finished dish still has too much liquid, boil it over high heat (or use the browning setting of an electric model), uncovered, for a few minutes to reduce the volume to desired consistency. You could also thicken the sauce with a bit of flour or cornstarch; remove some liquid from the cooker, stir in about ½ tablespoon flour or cornstarch for every 2 tablespoons of liquid, dissolve, and add the mixture back to the pot.

Some seasonings, including fresh herbs, parsley, and garlic, will dissipate more in a pressure cooker than in other cooking methods. Taste the finished dish to see if a little more needs to be added.

For additional guidance, consult recipes throughout this book that are similar to the one you want to adapt.

Use the following estimated cooking times as a starting point when adapting your favorite poultry recipes to the pressure cooker. Remember that the pressure cooker will yield poultry with uncrisped skin, much like stewing. You can cook with or without the skin, although we generally prefer to skin the chicken after cooking, because leaving the skin on tends to help maintain moisture. Always use at least the minimum amount of water recommended by your pressure cooker's manufacturer (the amount needed will vary for different models). After cooking, check with an instant-read thermometer to make sure that the poultry is cooked to an internal temperature of 170F (75C). If not, re-lock the cooker, bring back to pressure, and cook for a few more minutes.

Cooking Poultry in the Pressure Cooker

TYPE OF POULTRY	PRESSURE TO USE	MINUTES COOKED
Chicken, about 3 pounds		
Whole	High	15–20
Quartered	Low	15–17
Cut-up	Low	13–15
Split breasts, on-bone	Low	11–12
Whole legs	High	10–12
Thighs, on-bone	Low	10–12
Breast or thigh cut into 1-inch cubes or strips	High	2–3
or	Low	3–4
Cornish hens, whole	High	10–12
Duck, 4½ to 5 pounds		
Whole	High	25–30
Cut-up	High	13–15
Legs	Low	15–20
Turkey breast, 5 to 6 pounds	Low	40–45

The estimated cooking times are offered to help you adapt favorite family recipes for meat dishes to the pressure cooker. Cook at high pressure. Always use at least the minimum amount of water recommended by your pressure cooker's manufacturer (the amount needed

Cooking Meat in the Pressure Cooker

TYPE OF MEAT	MINUTES COOKED
Beef	
Brisket, about 3 pounds	50–60
Chuck roast, about 3 pounds	65–75
Corned beef, about 3 pounds	60–75
Oxtails, about 2 pounds	40–45
Ribs, about 3 pounds	25–30
Shanks, about 8 ounces each	30–35
Short ribs, about 3 pounds	30–35
Sirloin tip roast, about 2 pounds	15–17 (rare)
Stew meat, 1-inch cubes	15–18
Tongue, about 3 pounds	50–60
Lamb	
Shanks, about 12 ounces each	25–30
Stew meat, 1 inch cubes	12–15
Pork	
Chops, about 6 ounces each	8–10
Loin roast, about 2 pounds	18–22
Shoulder or butt roast, about 3 pounds	38–42
Spareribs, about 3 pounds	20–25
Rabbit, cut-up, about 3 pounds	25–30
Veal	
Breast, about 3 pounds	60–70
Kidney, about 1 pound	10–12
Roast, about 3 pounds	40–45
Shanks, about 8 ounces each	25–27
Stew meat, 1-inch cubes	8–10

will vary for different models). Also read your manufacturer's directions for specific instructions regarding the degree of heat over which the cooker should be brought to pressure; in some models, fattier cuts of meat being cooked in thick sauces should be brought to pressure over a temperate heat to prevent scorching. After cooking, check to make sure that the meat is cooked thoroughly. If not, recover the cooker, bring back to pressure, and cook for a few more minutes.

Use the estimated cooking times when adapting your own recipes for seafood stews and casseroles to the pressure cooker. Use high pressure and always add at least the minimum amount of water recommended by your pressure cooker's manufacturer (the amount needed will vary for different models). When cooking very thin fish fillets (less than ½ inch thick), wrap the fillet in parchment or in a leaf of chard or savoy cabbage to help keep it intact.

Pressure Cooking Times for Seafood

Cooking Seafood in the Pressure Cooker

TYPE OF SEAFOOD	MINUTES COOKED
Clams, in their shells*	1–2
Crab, hard-shell blue or Dungeness, whole	2–3
Fish	
Fillets	3–5
Steaks, 1 to 2 inches thick	2–4
Whole, 1 to 2 pounds	4–6
Lobster, 1¼ to 2 pounds, whole	2–3
Monkfish, 2 to 2½-inch cubes	2–4
Mussels, in their shells*	2–3
Octopus, whole baby or 3-inch pieces	14–16
Sea scallops*	1–2
Shrimp, with or without shells	1–2
Squid, ¾- to 1-inch rings	14–16

*Shelled clams and mussels and tiny bay scallops are too delicate to pressure cook; when you want to add them to a dish, do so after the pressure has lowered and cook over gentle heat or use the browning setting of an electric cooker.

Start checking for desired doneness at the lower end of the time ranges given, because seafood can be overcooked easily in a pressure cooker. When cooking most types of seafood, you will want to lower the pressure by a quick-release method; for such longer cooking varieties as squid and octopus, remove the cooker from the heat and allow the pressure to drop naturally. When a recipe calls for adding flour or cornstarch to thicken a sauce, stir it in over medium-low heat (or using the browning setting with an electric model) after the pressure has been lowered, to prevent scorching.

Soups and Stocks

From simple, but magically medicinal chicken soup with noodles to a complex mélange of root vegetables in incredibly rich beef broth, soups truly are food for the spirit as well as the flesh. They banish the chill of a wintry blast, spreading a glowing warmth from inside out.

And with a pressure cooker, flavorful fresh soups can be made from scratch in a manner of minutes. You'll be ladling up Chicken Noodle Soup in 6 minutes and Beef and Root Vegetable Soup in 12 minutes. Chicken–Wild Rice Soup takes all of 20 minutes, while New England–style Clam Chowder is ready in a mere 4 minutes.

You can even make soups using such typically long-cooking ingredients as pumpkin, butternut and acorn squash, beans ("soaking" the beans in the cooker takes 2 to 3 minutes), and chickpeas, which emerge from a single pressure cooker perfectly cooked in 12 to 25 minutes (12 minutes for Butternut Squash and White Bean Soup; 25 minutes for Chickpea Soup). In fact, we've been on a crusade to get everyone we know to start making soups in the pressure cooker; the only complaint we've received in response is from a friend who misses the lingering household aroma that comes from having stock-pots simmering on her stovetop for hours at a time.

For pureed soups, such as Pumpkin Cheese Soup, transfer the mixture to a food processor or blender or puree right in the cooker using a hand-held immersible blender.

Pressure cooker stocks are so wonderfully rich and quick to make— from 15 minutes for Fish Stock to 30 minutes for Beef Stock to 45 minutes for Chicken Stock—that we think you'll end up using your own homemade stocks as the basis for soup much of the time. (If you do start with canned stock be sure to taste before adding salt.)

Remember that different types of pressure cookers give off varying amounts of steam as they cook, which has a particularly pronounced effect on stock yields. An old-fashioned jiggle-top cooker, for example, will lose up to a cup in volume, whereas a spring-valve or electric model may actually extract sufficient moisture from bones and vegetables to increase the volume a bit.

Santa Fe Squash and Chicken Soup

Squash is one of those foods that just takes naturally to the pressure cooker. Not only is the squash for this soup cooked in 12 minutes instead of the usual 45 to 60 minutes but it holds its shape perfectly and comes out of the cooker succulent and sweet. Chipotle chiles— smoked jalapeños by another name—are a primary flavoring component of this Southwestern medley. They are available only canned in most parts of the country; look in your supermarket's Latin foods section. Garnish with Tortilla Strips (see below), if desired.

ELECTRIC
COMPATIBLE

MAKES 6 SERVINGS

1 (1-pound) acorn squash, peeled, seeded, and cut into 1 × ¼-inch pieces

1 bunch green onions, trimmed to white and light green parts, and sliced crosswise (about ½ cup)

½ cup corn kernels, preferably fresh

1 pound skinless, boneless chicken breasts, cut into 1 × ¼-inch pieces

1 canned chipotle chile, cored, seeded, deveined, and chopped (about 1 tablespoon)

1 teaspoon dried oregano

1 teaspoon ground coriander

2 cups defatted Chicken Stock (page 36 or canned)

1 tablespoon lime juice

½ teaspoon fresh grated lime zest

2 tablespoons chopped fresh cilantro

1 clove garlic, minced or peeled

Combine the squash, green onions, corn, chicken, chipotle chile, oregano, coriander, and stock in a pressure cooker. Cover, lock, and bring to high pressure over high heat. Reduce the heat to stabilize pressure and cook for 12 minutes.

Lower the pressure by a quick-release method. Carefully remove the cover and stir in the lime juice, lime zest, and cilantro. Stir in the minced garlic or press in a whole clove.

Tortilla Strips

This soup is especially good garnished with baked tortilla strips. Cut 2 or 3 corn tortillas into thin strips and scatter the strips on a non-stick baking sheet. Bake in a preheated 350F (175C) oven until golden, 6 to 8 minutes, tossing halfway through.

Chicken and Sausage Gumbo

**ELECTRIC
COMPATIBLE**
with Revision:

Use the browning setting to toast the flour and brown the vegetables.

We all love to eat our way around town when visiting New Orleans, but most of us would be as big as a bayou if we ate like that all the time. This quick, low-fat gumbo has all the flavor of the original—but by first toasting the flour, we're adding the flavor of a roux without the usual butter, drippings, or fat. Browning the okra cuts down on its natural viscosity. Gumbo filé powder, a traditional flavor component of gumbos and other Creole dishes, is made from sassafras leaves; look for it in your supermarket's spice section.

MAKES 10 SERVINGS

3 tablespoons all-purpose flour

8 ounces okra, trimmed, and cut into $\frac{1}{2}$-inch rounds (about $1\frac{3}{4}$ cups)

1 large green bell pepper, diced (about $1\frac{1}{2}$ cups)

1 large red bell pepper, diced (about $1\frac{1}{2}$ cups)

1 medium yellow onion, diced (about $1\frac{1}{4}$ cups)

2 medium stalks celery, diced (about $\frac{3}{4}$ cup)

6 cups defatted Chicken Stock (page 36 or canned) or Smoked Turkey Stock (page 38)

4 ounces ham steak, trimmed and cut into $\frac{1}{4}$-inch cubes

8 ounces smoked turkey sausage, cut into $\frac{1}{4}$-inch rounds

2 (6- to 7-ounce) skinless, boneless chicken breasts, cut into $1\frac{1}{2} \times \frac{1}{2}$-inch strips

1 ($14\frac{1}{2}$-ounce) can diced tomatoes

³/₄ cup long-grain white rice

2 tablespoons Italian seasoning

1 tablespoon Creole Seasoning (page 77 or purchased)

¹/₂ tablespoon gumbo filé powder

2 cloves garlic, minced or peeled

Put the flour into a pressure cooker. Stirring constantly, cook over medium-high heat until it begins to turn an even dark tan, 6 to 7 minutes. Add the okra and cook until the okra is lightly browned, about 1 minute. Add the bell peppers, onion, and celery. Cook, stirring, just to coat the vegetables, 10 to 15 seconds. Add the stock and stir to dislodge any browned bits stuck to the bottom of the cooker. Add the ham, sausage, and chicken. Stir well, making sure all the flour has dissolved. Stir in the tomatoes, rice, Italian seasoning, and Creole Seasoning. Cover, lock, and bring to high pressure over high heat. Reduce the heat to stabilize pressure and cook for 6 minutes.

Lower the pressure by a quick-release method. Carefully remove the cover and stir in the gumbo filé. Stir in the minced garlic or press in whole cloves.

Beef and Root Vegetable Soup

The pressure cooker coaxes an incredibly rich taste from the combination of beef and beef stock in this recipe, against which the flavors of the root vegetables really shine—the parsnips with a texture and taste a bit like a sweet white potato, the rutabaga and turnip firmer fleshed and earthier. Together, they provide a wonderfully complex medley of tastes and textures. Remember to peel the waxy coating off the rutabaga before chopping.

MAKES 8 SERVINGS

12 ounces beef round, trimmed and diced

2 medium stalks celery, chopped (about ¾ cup)

3 medium carrots, peeled and chopped (about 1 cup)

1 medium parsnip, peeled and chopped (about 1 cup)

2 medium turnips, chopped (about 1 cup)

1 medium rutabaga, peeled and chopped (about 1 cup)

1 medium yellow onion, chopped (about ¾ cup)

4 cups defatted Beef Stock (page 41 or canned)

2 sprigs fresh thyme

1 bay leaf

½ teaspoon salt

¼ teaspoon ground black pepper

¼ cup chopped fresh parsley

Combine all the ingredients, except the parsley, in a pressure cooker. Cover, lock, and bring to high pressure over high heat. Reduce the heat to stabilize pressure and cook for 12 minutes.

Remove the pressure cooker from the heat and let the pressure drop naturally. Carefully remove the cover and discard the thyme and bay leaf. Stir in the parsley.

Red Pepper and Corn Chowder

Use fresh corn in this creamy chowder if at all possible, or frozen and thawed corn in a pinch—never canned. For a smoky flavor without bacon, replace the Chicken Stock with Smoked Turkey Stock (page 38). For a low-fat chowder, substitute evaporated skim milk or one of the new nonfat half-and-half products for the heavy cream, or skip the heavy cream altogether and puree all of the soup rather than just half.

MAKES 4 SERVINGS

4 strips bacon, chopped

1 medium yellow onion, diced (about 1 cup)

3 cups corn kernels, preferably fresh (about 5 ears)

2 cups defatted Chicken Stock (page 36 or canned)

1/2 teaspoon ground cumin

1/2 teaspoon dried thyme or 1/2 tablespoon fresh thyme

1/4 teaspoon ground white pepper

1/2 cup heavy cream

2/3 cup chopped red bell pepper

1 tablespoon chopped fresh parsley

Put the bacon into a pressure cooker over medium heat. Stirring, cook just until crisp, 4 to 5 minutes. Remove the bacon and set it aside. Add the onion to the cooker and cook, stirring, until golden, about 1 1/2 minutes. Add the corn, stock, cumin, thyme, and white pepper. Cover, lock, and bring to high pressure over high heat. Reduce the heat to stabilize pressure and cook for 5 minutes.

Lower the pressure by a quick-release method. Carefully remove the cover. Puree 3 cups of the soup in a food processor or blender and return the puree to the cooker, along with the cream, bell pepper, and parsley. Heat just until steaming. Garnish each serving with a bit of bacon.

ELECTRIC COMPATIBLE
with Revision:

Use the browning setting to cook the bacon and then the onion. Serve the soup after pureeing, without reheating.

STRIPPING FRESH CORN

Don't be deterred by the thought of starting with fresh corn on the cob—removing the kernels takes barely more time than unwrapping and opening a box of frozen corn kernels! First, shuck the husk and silk. Stand the ear upright and slice down with a sharp knife, releasing the kernels; rotate and repeat all around the cob, or fit the cob with a serrated-collar corn stripper and release all the kernels at once by pushing down firmly.

ELECTRIC
COMPATIBLE
with Revision:

In the first step, use the browning setting to bring the water and bean combination to a gentle boil. After initially cooking the beans, lower the pressure using the quick-release button.

Butternut Squash and White Bean Soup

Pressure cooking dried beans for 2 to 3 minutes before beginning the other recipe steps eliminates the need to soak the beans overnight and is considerably quicker than even the old-fashioned "quick-soak" method of boiling for 5 minutes and then letting the pot sit off the heat, covered, for 1 hour. In this recipe, it also serves the purpose of precooking the beans a bit, because they take longer to cook than the squash. Navy beans, Great Northern beans, or any white bean could easily be substituted for the cannellini beans. We especially like this dish made with our Brown Chicken Stock, which lends a somewhat deep, rich flavor.

MAKES 4 SERVINGS

$\frac{1}{2}$ cup dried cannellini beans

3 large cloves garlic, peeled, plus 1 additional clove, minced

1 bay leaf

2 cups water

6 ounces leek, trimmed to white and light green parts, chopped (about $\frac{2}{3}$ cup), and rinsed well

1 (8-ounce) butternut squash, peeled, and chopped (about $1\frac{1}{4}$ cups)

1 medium stalk celery, chopped (about $\frac{1}{3}$ cup)

1 large carrot, peeled and chopped (about $\frac{1}{2}$ cup)

1 tablespoon olive oil

4 cups Brown Chicken Stock (page 37), defatted Chicken Stock (page 36 or canned), or canned vegetable stock

$\frac{1}{2}$ teaspoon dried sage

$\frac{1}{4}$ teaspoon ground white pepper

$\frac{1}{4}$ teaspoon dried thyme

2 tablespoons chopped fresh parsley

Salt, to taste

Combine the beans, 2 whole cloves garlic, the bay leaf, and water in a pressure cooker. Bring to a boil over high heat. Cover, lock, and bring to high pressure. Reduce the heat to stabilize pressure and cook for 2 minutes.

Lower the pressure by the cold water–release method. Carefully remove the cover. Drain and set aside the beans, discarding the bay leaf. When the pressure cooker is cool enough to handle, rinse and dry it.

Combine the leek, squash, celery, carrot, oil, and minced garlic in the cooker over medium-high heat. Cook until the leek begins to brown, 1½ to 2 minutes. Add the beans, stock, sage, pepper, and thyme. Cover, lock, and bring to high pressure over high heat. Reduce the heat to stabilize pressure and cook for 12 minutes.

Remove the pressure cooker from the heat and let the pressure drop naturally. Carefully remove the cover, stir in the parsley and salt to taste; press in the remaining clove garlic.

Chickpea Soup

Also called garbanzo beans, nutritious chickpeas have been popular since ancient times among peoples of the Mediterranean basin. Although chickpeas normally take over 2 hours to cook, they emerge from the pressure cooker in less than half an hour—tender and reasonably uniform in texture, a novelty for the sometimes stubbornly erratic legume. Although you could serve the soup with all the beans intact or puree the whole yield, we're partial to the juxtaposition of some still slightly crunchy whole chickpeas floating in pureed stock.

MAKES 6 SERVINGS

1 pound dried chickpeas (about 4 cups), picked over

6 cups water

6 cups defatted Chicken Stock (page 36 or canned)

1 large yellow onion, chopped (about 1½ cups)

2 large carrots, peeled and chopped (about 1 cup)

3 medium stalks celery, chopped (about 1 cup)

1 (14½-ounce) can diced tomatoes

2 slices bacon, chopped

2 large cloves garlic, minced

1 tablespoon chopped fresh rosemary

½ teaspoon salt

¼ teaspoon ground black pepper

Combine the chickpeas and water in a pressure cooker. Cover, lock, and bring to high pressure over high heat. Reduce the heat to stabilize pressure and cook for 2 minutes.

Lower the pressure by a quick-release method. Carefully remove the cover. Drain the chickpeas and return them to the cooker. Add the stock, onion, carrots, celery, tomatoes, and bacon. Cover, lock, and bring to high pressure over high heat. Reduce the heat to stabilize pressure and cook for 25 minutes.

Lower the pressure by a quick-release method. Carefully remove the cover. Puree half of the soup in a food processor or blender and return it to the cooker. Stir in the garlic, rosemary, salt, and pepper.

Chicken Noodle Soup

This is a feel-good soup that's sure to please the kids in your household as well as the adults. Ann Bloomstrand, our frequent comrade in projects culinary, took some home after one of our cooking binges and, much to her delight, found it in the freezer—the soup freezes beautifully—a month or two later when she was laid up with the flu. We like to think the soup had something to do with her swift recovery. Cook the pasta separately and stir it into the soup; it would give off too much starch if you cooked it with the other ingredients in the pressure cooker.

 ELECTRIC COMPATIBLE

MAKES 6 SERVINGS

12 ounces skinless, boneless chicken breast, diced

2 medium carrots, peeled and diced (about ¾ cup)

2 medium stalks celery, diced (about ⅔ cup)

1 small yellow onion, diced (about ¾ cup)

1 clove garlic, minced

½ teaspoon poultry seasoning

3½ cups defatted Chicken Stock (page 36 or canned)

1 cup small bow-tie pasta (farfalline)

½ teaspoon salt

Combine the chicken, carrots, celery, onion, garlic, poultry seasoning, and stock in a pressure cooker. Cover, lock, and bring to high pressure over high heat. Reduce the heat to stabilize pressure and cook for 6 minutes.

Meanwhile, bring water to a boil in a medium saucepan. Add the pasta and cook until al dente, about 4 minutes.

Lower the pressure by a quick-release method. Carefully remove the cover. Drain the pasta and stir it into the soup, along with the salt.

ELECTRIC
COMPATIBLE
with Revision:

*Use the browning setting to
cook the bacon and then
the vegetables. After
pressure cooking, use the
browning setting to whisk
in the flour mixture.*

Clam Chowder

**This is classic milky-white New England clam chowder, not the red-
dish chowder of Manhattan fame. You could start with homemade fish
stock or the commercial frozen fish stock available in better markets;
or use all clam juice (about 4½ cups) instead of a mixture of fish
stock and clam juice. If you prefer to use fresh clams, you will need
1 cup chopped.**

MAKES 8 SERVINGS

4 slices bacon, diced

2 medium stalks celery, diced (about ⅔ cup)

1 medium yellow onion, diced (about 1⅓ cups)

3 cups Fish Stock (page 40 or frozen)

3 (6½-ounce) cans chopped clams, drained, juice reserved

2 medium baking potatoes (about 12 ounces total), scrubbed
and diced

½ teaspoon dried thyme, or ½ tablespoon fresh thyme

2 tablespoons all-purpose flour

½ cup half-and-half

2 tablespoons chopped fresh parsley

1 teaspoon salt

¼ teaspoon ground black pepper

Put the bacon into a pressure cooker over medium-low heat. Cook
until beginning to brown, 4 to 5 minutes. Add the celery and onion and
cook until the onion turns translucent, about 2 minutes. Add the
stock, reserved clam juice, potatoes, and thyme. Cover, lock, and bring
to high pressure over high heat. Reduce the heat to stabilize pressure
and cook for 4 minutes. Meanwhile, whisk together the flour and half-
and-half in a small bowl.

Lower the pressure by a quick-release method. Carefully remove the
cover. Over medium-high heat, whisk in the flour mixture. Continue to
whisk until thickened, about 2 minutes, then bring to a boil. Remove the
cooker from the heat and stir in the clams, parsley, salt, and pepper.

Caramelized Five-Onion Soup

More complex than most onion soups, this rendition boasts shallots and leek in addition to red, yellow, and white onions. If you want to use a single variety of onion instead, we suggest about 2 pounds of Vidalia onions. The natural sweetness of the onions gets a boost in the recipe from caramelization and the addition of a bit of balsamic vinegar.

MAKES 6 SERVINGS

2 tablespoons olive oil

1 large white onion, sliced (about 2 cups)

1 medium red onion, sliced (about 1⅓ cups)

1 medium yellow onion, sliced (about 1⅓ cups)

1 large or 2 small shallots, sliced (about ½ cup)

8 ounces leek, trimmed to white and light green parts, sliced (about 1¼ cups), and rinsed well

2 cloves garlic, minced

2 tablespoons sugar

1 tablespoon balsamic vinegar

1 teaspoon dried thyme

3½ cups defatted Beef Stock (page 41 or canned)

6 Garlic Cheese Croutons (see below)

Preheat a pressure cooker over medium heat and swirl in the oil. Add the onions, shallots, leek, and garlic. Cook, stirring occasionally, until the onions have wilted, about 10 minutes. Add the sugar and vinegar. Cook, stirring occasionally, until the onions are well caramelized, about 20 minutes.

Add the thyme and stock. Cover, lock, and bring to high pressure over high heat. Reduce the heat to stabilize pressure and cook for 10 minutes.

Remove the pressure cooker from the heat and let the pressure drop naturally. Carefully remove the cover. Serve about 1 cup per person, ladled over a crouton.

ELECTRIC COMPATIBLE

with Revision:

When caramelizing the onions, if your cooker can be set to preheat/brown for only 20 minutes, reprogram it for an additional 20 minutes on the browning setting after adding the sugar and vinegar.

CLEANING LEEKS

Always rinse leeks, which can contain a lot of residual grit, well—trim off all the dark green parts, cut the leek in half lengthwise, slice crosswise and then put into a colander, rinse under cold running water, and drain well.

Garlic Cheese Croutons

These can also be served with other soups or a salad.

6 slices French bread

6 tablespoons shredded Gruyère cheese

2 cloves garlic, minced

1 tablespoon freshly grated Parmesan cheese

Preheat the broiler. Toast the French bread on 1 side in the broiler. Turn the slices over and scatter 1 tablespoon of the Gruyère on each. Sprinkle garlic and Parmesan on top and return to the broiler until the Gruyère has melted.

Lentil Soup

ELECTRIC
COMPATIBLE
with Revision:

Use the browning setting to cook the bacon and the vegetables.

In many traditional lentil soup recipes, the vegetables are first cooked over very low heat for about 30 minutes; then the lentils are added and the mixture is cooked for another 45 minutes or so. Here, the soup is made from start to finish in 16 minutes. For salads, we usually look for the small, dark French green lentils, which hold their crunch nicely when cooked. For soup making, however, the common variety sold in every supermarket, which are softer, work better.

MAKES 6 SERVINGS

2 slices thick-cut bacon, chopped

2 medium stalks celery, chopped (about ⅔ cup)

1 medium carrot, peeled and chopped (about ⅓ cup)

1 large yellow onion, chopped (about 1½ cups)

3 plum tomatoes, seeded and chopped (about 1 cup)

4 ounces ham steak, trimmed and chopped

1½ cups dried lentils, picked over and rinsed

4 cups defatted Chicken Stock (page 36 or canned)

1 teaspoon dried thyme or 1 tablespoon fresh thyme

2 large cloves garlic, minced or peeled

Preheat a pressure cooker over high heat. Add the bacon and cook, stirring constantly, until browned, 2 to 3 minutes. Add the celery, carrot, and onion and cook, stirring constantly, until the onion has softened, about 2 minutes. Stir in the tomatoes, ham, lentils, and stock. Cover, lock, and bring to high pressure over high heat. Reduce the heat to stabilize pressure and cook for 11 minutes.

Remove the pressure cooker from the heat and let the pressure drop naturally. Carefully remove the cover. Stir in the thyme. Stir in minced garlic or press in whole cloves.

Chicken–Wild Rice Soup

**We love the naturally distinctive crunch of wild rice, which is all too
often lost to overcooking. Cooked, wild rice should be tender but still
firm, each grain swollen and just slightly split open, not butterflied as
some would argue. We have timed the recipe for long-grain wild rice,
which has a fairly high moisture content and will thus cook quickly.
Mature portobello mushrooms could be substituted for the baby por-
tobellos, also known as creminis. Clean the mushrooms with a mush-
room brush or a cloth, or rinse and dry them; there's nothing wrong
with gently rinsing most mushrooms, just don't let them soak.**

MAKES 4 SERVINGS

4 ounces baby portobello mushrooms, cleaned, stemmed, and
chopped (about 1¼ cups)

4 ounces white button mushrooms, cleaned, stemmed, and
chopped (about 1¼ cups)

8 ounces leek, trimmed to white and light green parts, sliced
(about 1 cup), and well rinsed

¾ cup corn kernels, preferably fresh

½ cup wild rice, very well rinsed

6 ounces skinless, boneless chicken breast, cubed

2 cups defatted Chicken Stock (page 36 or canned) or Brown
Chicken Stock (page 37)

2 tablespoons chopped fresh parsley

½ teaspoon salt

¼ teaspoon ground black pepper

Combine the mushrooms, leek, corn, rice, chicken, and stock in a pressure cooker. Cover, lock, and bring to low pressure over high heat.
Reduce the heat to stabilize pressure and cook for 20 minutes. (Cook
at high pressure for 15 minutes if you have a model that only works at
high pressure.)

Remove the pressure cooker from the heat and let the pressure
drop naturally. Carefully remove the cover and stir in the parsley, salt,
and pepper.

Yellow Split-Pea Soup

Not a vegetarian dish, this soup derives much of its flavor from the ham bone and scraps or the ham hock with which the vegetables cook. (Fresh ham hock is preferable to smoked; if you use a smoked hock, don't add any salt.) Green split peas would work every bit as well as the yellow variety, which we just happened to have on hand when we made split-pea soup in Duck, North Carolina, one year with the remains of the Christmas ham. As split-pea soup tends to thicken quite a bit as it sets, you may want to add ½ to 1 cup water or stock to the soup when you reheat it.

ELECTRIC
COMPATIBLE

MAKES 8 SERVINGS

2 small yellow onions, chopped (about 1¾ cups)

2 large carrots, peeled and chopped (about 1 cup)

3 large stalks celery, chopped (about 1¼ cups)

1 (1-pound) ham bone with some scraps of meat or ham hock

1 pound dried yellow split peas (about 2⅓ cups), picked over

6 cups water

¾ teaspoon dried thyme or 2 teaspoons chopped fresh thyme

½ teaspoon ground black pepper

¼ teaspoon salt

Combine the onions, carrots, celery, ham bone, split peas, and water in a pressure cooker. Cover, lock, and bring to high pressure over high heat. Reduce the heat to stabilize pressure and cook for 12 minutes.

Remove the pressure cooker from the heat and let the pressure drop naturally. Carefully remove the cover. Take the ham bone or ham hock out of the cooker and stir the remaining ingredients well. Cut the meat off the bone, chop it, and return to the cooker. Stir in the thyme, pepper, and salt.

ELECTRIC
COMPATIBLE
with Revision:

*Use the browning setting
for the final ingredient
additions after pureeing the
soup.*

Pumpkin Cheese Soup

**Ever wonder what to do with the meat from the Halloween jack-o'-
lantern? Try this rich, velvety soup. Making it in the pressure cooker
cuts down considerably on preparation time, because the pumpkin
meat would otherwise have to be boiled for almost an eternity to be
edible. The soup can be made with Chicken Stock, but it is particularly good with Smoked Turkey Stock, the smokiness of the stock providing a nice contrast to the natural sweetness of the pumpkin.**

MAKES 8 SERVINGS

1 (2-pound) pumpkin, peeled, seeded, and cut into chunks

1 medium white onion, cut into chunks

1½ cups Smoked Turkey Stock (page 38), Turkey Stock (page
38), or defatted Chicken Stock (page 36 or canned)

½ teaspoon ground allspice

1 cup skim milk

1 teaspoon mild Curry Powder (see below or purchased)

½ teaspoon salt

¼ teaspoon ground white pepper

12 ounces white Cheddar cheese, grated (about 3 cups)

Combine the pumpkin, onion, stock, and allspice in a pressure cooker.
Cover, lock, and bring to high pressure over high heat. Reduce the heat
to stabilize pressure and cook for 12 minutes.

Lower the pressure by a quick-release method. Carefully remove
the cover and add the milk. Puree the soup using a hand-held
immersible blender or in a food processor or blender. Return the
cooker to medium heat. Stir in the curry powder, salt, and pepper; then
the cheese. Cook until the cheese has melted completely and the soup
is steamy.

Curry Powder

**A potent weapon in any cook's arsenal, curry powder of differing
strengths—from mild all the way up to Madras—can be the basis for a**

range of dishes with subtle but distinctive taste differences. Curry powders are actually mixtures of several spices. Use a fairly mild mixture such as this one to season the Pumpkin Cheese Soup or as a starting point for creating your own curries, varying the basic formula as your taste buds dictate. For a hotter curry, add up to ¼ teaspoon cayenne pepper.

MAKES ABOUT 6 TABLESPOONS

2 tablespoons ground coriander

1 tablespoon ground turmeric

1 tablespoon ground cumin

1 tablespoon celery seeds

1 teaspoon ground ginger

1 teaspoon ground cloves

¾ teaspoon ground black pepper

¾ teaspoon ground nutmeg

Mix together all the ingredients in a small bowl. Store in an airtight container.

Oxtail Soup

We're thrilled that cooks are rediscovering oxtails, long considered a throwaway cut by many. Well suited to moist, long-cooking methods of preparation, oxtails are a perfect match for the pressure cooker, emerging juicy, tender, and packed with flavor. The hearty soup we make from the resultant oxtail broth and meat is so rich that we usually prefer to start the recipe with blander canned beef broth rather than homemade stock. This soup is finished in the classical manner with a flourish of wine; we prefer Madeira, but you could use dry sherry or Marsala as well.

Sometimes we make the soup a day in advance, cover, and refrigerate overnight to allow the fat to rise to the top, facilitating the skimming.

ELECTRIC COMPATIBLE
with Revision:

If your cooker is a model that can be set to cook for only 30 minutes, reprogram it for an additional 15 minutes after the soup has cooked for 30 minutes.

1¾ pounds oxtails

2 (14½-ounce) cans beef broth

1 medium white onion, peeled

4 cloves garlic, peeled

1 tablespoon tomato paste

8 whole black peppercorns

¼ teaspoon celery seeds

3 medium stalks celery, diced (about 1 cup)

1 small yellow onion, diced (about ¾ cup)

1 large carrot, peeled and diced (about ½ cup)

¼ cup pearled barley

¼ cup chopped sun-dried tomatoes (dry pack)

¼ teaspoon dried thyme or ¾ teaspoon fresh thyme

¼ cup Madeira

¼ teaspoon salt

⅛ teaspoon ground black pepper

Combine the oxtails, broth, white onion, garlic, tomato paste, peppercorns, and celery seeds in a pressure cooker. Cover, lock, and bring to high pressure over high heat. Reduce the heat to stabilize pressure and cook for 45 minutes.

Lower the pressure by a quick-release method. Carefully remove the cover. Strain the stock into a large measuring cup or a bowl, skim the fat off the top, and return to the pressure cooker. Remove the meat from the bones, shred it, and add to the stock in the cooker, discarding the remaining contents of the strainer. Add the celery, yellow onion, carrot, barley, sun-dried tomatoes, and thyme. Cover, lock, and bring to high pressure over high heat. Reduce the heat to stabilize pressure and cook for 10 minutes.

Remove the pressure cooker from the heat and let the pressure drop naturally. Carefully remove the cover. Stir in the Madeira, salt, and pepper.

Basil, Barley, and Shiitake Soup

This hearty, cold-weather soup—a full meal in a bowl—is a blend of the traditional Italian flavor combination of basil and barley and the classic American pairing of basil and mushrooms. Long-cooking barley, which normally takes about 1 hour, is done in 20 minutes in the pressure cooker. For variety, replace the shiitakes with 1 ounce of dried Chinese black mushrooms that have been soaked for 20 minutes in hot water.

ELECTRIC
COMPATIBLE

MAKES 6 SERVINGS

2 medium stalks celery, diced (about ⅔ cup)

1 medium yellow onion, diced (about 1 cup)

1 large carrot, peeled and diced (about ½ cup)

2 teaspoons olive oil

4 cloves garlic, minced

12 ounces skinless, boneless chicken breast, roughly chopped

4 ounces shiitake mushrooms, cleaned, stemmed, and roughly chopped (about 1¼ cups)

4 cups defatted Chicken Stock (page 36 or canned) or Brown Chicken Stock (page 37)

½ cup pearled barley

⅓ cup chopped fresh basil

½ teaspoon ground black pepper

Salt to taste

Preheat a pressure cooker over medium heat. Add the celery, onion, carrot, and oil. Sauté until the onion is translucent, 2 to 3 minutes. Add the garlic and chicken. Increase the heat to high and cook, stirring constantly, until the chicken is no longer pink, about 1 minute. Stir in the shiitakes and stock. Bring to a boil, cook 5 to 7 minutes, then stir in the barley. Cover, lock, and bring to high pressure over high heat. Reduce the heat to stabilize pressure and cook for 20 minutes.

Lower the pressure by a quick-release method. Carefully remove the cover and stir in the basil. Cover and set aside for about 2 minutes, until the basil has wilted. Stir in the pepper and salt.

ELECTRIC
COMPATIBLE
with Revision:

*Reduce the amount of
chicken bones and scraps
used to 2½ pounds, reduce
the amount of water to 6
cups, and halve the
remaining ingredients. This
will yield 6 to 7 cups stock.*

Chicken Stock

**We use chicken stock constantly in a wide range of recipes—and the
pressure cooker allows us to make fresh, flavorful, and unadulterated
stock from scratch in a matter of minutes. Refrigerating the stock
overnight brings the fat to the top of the bowl, making skimming an
easy task. You will be able to lift most of the layer off with a large
spoon; afterward, scrape along the top with a dinner knife to catch
any residual bits of fat.**

MAKES ABOUT 9 CUPS

1 large yellow onion (unpeeled), cut into chunks

1 medium parsnip (unpeeled), cut into chunks

2 large stalks celery with leaves, cut into chunks

3 medium carrots (unpeeled), cut into chunks

4 pounds chicken bones with meat scraps

5 sprigs fresh parsley

6 whole black peppercorns

9 cups water

Combine all ingredients in a pressure cooker. Cover, lock, and bring to
high pressure over high heat. Reduce the heat to stabilize pressure and
cook for 45 minutes.

Remove the pressure cooker from the heat and let the pressure
drop naturally. Carefully remove the cover. Discard all the solid ingredients and strain the stock into a large bowl. Cover, refrigerate for at
least 2 hours, and then skim. To store, see page 38.

Brown Chicken Stock

A bit darker and richer-tasting than plain chicken stock, Brown
Chicken Stock makes for particularly good Basil, Barley, and Shiitake
Soup (page 35) and Veal Stew (page 59). Resist your initial urge to
peel when making stocks. (But do wash the vegetables first.) The
peels add flavor and will ultimately be strained out of the stock.
Rutabaga is the one exception; it is usually waxed and should therefore be peeled.

MAKES ABOUT 8 CUPS

ELECTRIC
COMPATIBLE
with Revision:

*Reduce the amount of
chicken bones and scraps
used to 3 pounds, reduce
the amount of water to 6
cups, and halve the
remaining ingredients. This
will yield about 6 cups
stock.*

  1 small celeriac root peeled and cut into chunks

  1 medium rutabaga, peeled and cut into chunks

  1 large yellow onion peeled and cut into chunks

  1 large carrot (unpeeled), halved

  1 medium parsnip (unpeeled), halved

  4 pounds chicken bones with meat scraps

  12 whole black peppercorns

  1 tablespoon fresh thyme or 1 teaspoon dried thyme

  8 cups water

Preheat the oven to 450F (230C).

Combine the celeriac root, rutabaga, onion, carrot, parsnip, and
chicken bones in a roasting pan. Roast for about 30 minutes, until well
browned.

Remove the browned vegetables and chicken bones to a pressure
cooker. Add the peppercorns, thyme, and water. Cover, lock, and bring
to high pressure over high heat. Reduce the heat to stabilize pressure
and cook for 40 minutes.

Remove the pressure cooker from the heat and let the pressure
drop naturally. Carefully remove the cover. Discard all solid ingredients and strain the stock into a large bowl. Cover, refrigerate for at
least 2 hours, and then skim. To store, see page 38.

ELECTRIC
COMPATIBLE
with Revision:

Reduce the amount of turkey bones and scraps used to $1^2/_3$ pounds, reduce the amount of water to 6 cups, and halve all remaining ingredients except the bay leaf. This will yield 6 to $6^1/_2$ cups stock.

STORING STOCK

Most homemade stocks will keep for 3 days in the refrigerator and up to 6 months in the freezer. We usually make them in quantity as time allows and then freeze in 2- and 4-cup portions in heavy-duty plastic storage bags so that we always have a supply on hand.

Turkey Stock

We use Turkey Stock to make the likes of White Chili (page 170) and Chile Verde Chili (page 138).

MAKES ABOUT 8 CUPS

1 medium white onion (unpeeled), cut into chunks

1 medium turnip (unpeeled), cut into chunks

2 medium stalks celery with leaves, cut into chunks

1 medium carrot (unpeeled), cut into chunks

$2^1/_2$ pounds turkey bones with meat scraps

12 whole black peppercorns

1 bay leaf

8 cups water

Combine all ingredients in a pressure cooker. Cover, lock, and bring to high pressure over high heat. Reduce the heat to stabilize pressure and cook for 40 minutes.

Remove the pressure cooker from the heat and let the pressure drop naturally. Carefully remove the cover. Discard all the solid ingredients and strain the stock into a large bowl. Cover, refrigerate for at least 2 hours, and then skim.

Smoked Turkey Stock

This rich, complex stock adds a new flavor dimension to a number of dishes, from Pumpkin Cheese Soup (page 32) to Chicken and Sausage Gumbo (page 18), Creole Crab and Rice Stew (page 118) to Cajun Red Beans and Rice (page 166). Use any smoked turkey bones with a little meat on them for the stock. If you don't have the remains of a smoked turkey on hand, look in your supermarket's poultry counter; most markets now carry packages of smoked turkey wings and necks.

MAKES ABOUT 9 CUPS

- 1 large stalk celery with leaves, cut into chunks
- 1 large carrot (unpeeled), cut into chunks
- 1 large yellow onion (unpeeled), cut into chunks
- 3 pounds smoked turkey bones with meat scraps
- 1 bay leaf
- 8¼ cups water

Combine all ingredients in a pressure cooker. Cover, lock, and bring to high pressure over high heat. Reduce the heat to stabilize pressure and cook for 35 minutes.

Remove the pressure cooker from the heat and let the pressure drop naturally. Carefully remove the cover. Discard all solid ingredients, including the bay leaf, and strain the stock into a large bowl. Cover, refrigerate for at least 2 hours, and then skim. To store, see page 38.

Duck Stock

Put the reserved neck, giblets, and wings from Duck Confit (page 87) to good use making this stock, an essential ingredient of Cassoulet (page 163).

MAKES ABOUT 6 CUPS

- 1 medium yellow onion (unpeeled), cut into chunks
- 2 large stalks celery with leaves, cut into chunks
- 3 medium carrots (unpeeled), cut into chunks
- 1¼ to 1½ pounds duck trimmings (wings, necks, and giblets)
- 12 whole black peppercorns
- 6 cups water

Combine all ingredients in a pressure cooker. Cover, lock, and bring to high pressure over high heat. Reduce the heat to stabilize pressure and cook for 35 minutes.

Remove the pressure cooker from the heat and let the pressure drop naturally. Carefully remove the cover. Discard all the solid ingredients and strain the stock into a large bowl. Cover, refrigerate for at least 2 hours, and then skim. To store, see page 38.

 ELECTRIC COMPATIBLE

Fish Stock

Fish stock, which is easily made at home and which can also be found in the freezer case of better supermarkets, is a component of a number of our seafood offerings, from Paella (page 152) to Clam Chowder (page 26) to Jamaican Squid (page 114). We usually ask our fishmonger for the head and bones when we have her fillet whole fish for us; we then freeze the parts for future fish stocks. With a day's notice or so, some fish markets will gladly sell you a supply as well.

MAKES ABOUT 5 CUPS

1½ pounds fish bones with heads and scraps

1 small white onion (unpeeled), quartered

1 clove garlic (unpeeled)

6 sprigs fresh parsley

6 whole black peppercorns

1 teaspoon fresh lemon juice

1 cup dry white wine

4 cups water

Combine all ingredients in a pressure cooker. Cover, lock, and bring to high pressure over high heat. Reduce the heat to stabilize pressure and cook for 15 minutes.

Remove the pressure cooker from the heat and let the pressure drop naturally. Carefully remove the cover. Discard all the solid ingredients and strain the stock into a large bowl. Cover, refrigerate for at least 2 hours, and then skim. To store, see page 38.

Beef Stock

Roasting the vegetables and beef bones for this stock produces a deep, dark color and a very rich taste. We use it constantly to enhance such dishes as Moroccan Lamb and Prune Tagine (page 73) and African Beef and Okra Stew (page 55).

MAKES ABOUT 8 CUPS

2 medium carrots (unpeeled), halved

2 medium stalks celery with leaves, halved

1 medium tomato, quartered, or 2 plum tomatoes, halved

1 large yellow onion, peeled and cut into 8 chunks

4 cloves garlic, peeled

5 pounds beef bones with meat scraps

1 cup dry red wine

8 whole black peppercorns

1 bay leaf

8 cups water

ELECTRIC COMPATIBLE *with Revision:*

Reduce the amount of beef bones and scraps used to 3 pounds, reduce the amount of water to 5 1/2 cups, reduce the amount of wine to 2/3 cup, and halve all remaining ingredients except the bay leaf. This will yield about 6 cups stock.

Preheat the oven to 450F (230C).

Put the carrots, celery, tomato, onion, garlic, and beef bones into a roasting pan. Roast for about 30 minutes or until the bones are very brown.

Remove the roasted beef bones and vegetables to a pressure cooker. Transfer the roasting pan to the stovetop and add the wine. Cook over high heat until reduced by about 75 percent, 5 to 6 minutes, stirring and scraping to dislodge any browned bits stuck to the pan.

Pour the contents of the pan over the bones and vegetables in the pressure cooker. Add the peppercorns, bay leaf, and water. Bring to a rapid boil over high heat and skim off the foamy residue that rises to the top. Cover, lock, and bring to high pressure over high heat. Reduce the heat to stabilize pressure and cook for 30 minutes.

Remove the pressure cooker from the heat and let the pressure drop naturally. Carefully remove the cover. Discard all solid ingredients, including the bay leaf, and strain the stock into a large bowl. Cover, refrigerate for at least 2 hours, and then skim. To store, see page 38.

Meats

Even before we became admitted "pressure cooker junkies," we knew the cookers were especially good at tenderizing inexpensive, long-cooking cuts of meat—the cooking method of choice for shanks and stews of all sorts, for getting the best out of brisket or pacifying pot roast. We've since learned the true range of meats that benefit from pressure cooking.

Yes, Lamb Shanks with Rosemary and Green Olives, prepared in 25 minutes in the pressure cooker, is delightful, as is Veal Stew, ready in 13 minutes. Southwestern Brisket and German Pot Roast take a bit longer—60 and 75 minutes, respectively—but emerge from the cooker tender and juicy.

The star of our trials, however was Asian Roast Beef, a rare and robust sirloin tip accented with lemon grass, ginger, and soy, that took but 16 minutes to prepare. The pressure cooker also yielded the leanest (but still moist) Classic Corned Beef we've ever tasted and a real, old-fashioned, fork-tender Veal Breast (the kind that can cook all Sunday afternoon on the stovetop and still be a bit chewy)! Our recipes range the butcher's block from Russian Lamb and Artichokes (10 minutes) to Bourbon Pork Roast (15 minutes), and Pistachio Country Pâté made from a turkey and ham mixture (20 minutes) to

Meaty Chili made with beef and pork (20 minutes), and Barbecue Spareribs (25 minutes) to Oxtail Stew (40 minutes).

Cook dishes with very thick sauces, such as Texas Chili Beef Ribs, Spring Lamb Stew, and African Beef and Okra Stew, at low pressure if your cooker has a low pressure setting. In most beef and pork recipes, we call for lowering the pressure naturally so as not to risk toughening the meat.

Southwestern Brisket

The first time we tasted real barbecue beef brisket it was, as the old punch line goes, love at first bite. The setting was Sonny Bryan's in Dallas—the original smokehouse shack downtown—a ramshackle structure with a take-out counter and a few battered old school desks should anyone want to chow down on site. When we called there one Saturday morning to ask how late they stayed open, the reply was, "Until we're sold out." Generally, we would soon learn to our sometimes late-rising chagrin, this is well before noon on weekends. Finding Sonny's still stocked on our second foray at an earlier hour, we bought several pounds of brisket with the best intentions of dropping a generous portion off later that day at the Chicago home of the food writers who had told us about the smokehouse. Half of the heavenly provisions actually made it to the airport; but the airline rations were so depressing, they drove us straight to the rest of the stash.

ELECTRIC
COMPATIBLE
with Revision:

If your cooker is a model that can be set to cook for only 30 minutes, reprogram it for an additional 30 minutes after the brisket has cooked for 30 minutes. Use the browning setting to bring the sauce to a gentle boil for simmering the sliced brisket.

MAKES 8 SERVINGS

1 small yellow onion, minced (about ¾ cup)

1 cup tomato sauce

¼ cup cider vinegar

2 cloves garlic, minced

¼ cup firmly packed light brown sugar

½ tablespoon dry mustard

1 teaspoon ground coriander

1 teaspoon hot paprika

1 teaspoon salt

¾ teaspoon ground cumin

¼ teaspoon ground turmeric

1 teaspoon mesquite-flavored Liquid Smoke

1 (2¾- to 3-pound) beef brisket, visible fat removed

Combine all the ingredients, except the brisket, in a pressure cooker. Stir to mix. Add the brisket, spooning sauce over to coat. Cover, lock, and bring to high pressure over medium-high heat. Reduce the heat to stabilize pressure and cook for 60 minutes.

Remove the pressure cooker from the heat and let the pressure drop naturally. Carefully remove the cover and transfer the meat to a cutting board. Over medium heat, bring the sauce in the cooker to a boil and boil for 5 minutes. Thinly slice the meat across the grain and return it to the pressure cooker. Simmer for 5 minutes.

Classic Corned Beef

ELECTRIC
COMPATIBLE
with Revision:

If your cooker is a model that can be set to cook for only 30 minutes, reprogram it for an additional 30 minutes after the brisket has cooked for 30 minutes. Then reprogram it for another 15 minutes.

You don't have to be Irish and it doesn't have be St. Patrick's Day to savor this lean corned beef. Equally good sliced thin and piled between slices of good rye bread, corned beef prepared in a pressure cooker is among the leanest we've ever tasted, but still moist and fla-vorful. Even better is that the typically all-afternoon job of cooking the corned beef is reduced to a little over 1 hour. Select a brisket that is even in thickness all the way across so that it will cook evenly.

For the classic potato and cabbage accompaniment, remove the brisket from the cooker and add a quartered head of green cabbage and 2 peeled and quartered large potatoes. Cover, lock, and bring back to high pressure over high heat. Reduce the heat to stabilize pressure and cook for 2 minutes. Lower the pressure by a quick-release method.

MAKES 6 TO 8 SERVINGS

1 (3-pound) corned beef brisket

2 tablespoons pickling spice

2 cloves garlic, peeled

1 bay leaf

4 cups water

Put the corned beef into a pressure cooker, along with any juices from the bag in which it was sealed. Sprinkle the pickling spice on top. Add the garlic, bay leaf, and water to the cooker. Cover, lock, and bring to high pressure over high heat. Reduce the heat to stabilize pressure and cook for 75 minutes.

Remove the pressure cooker from the heat and let the pressure drop naturally. Carefully remove the cover. Remove the meat and thinly slice it against the grain.

Reuben Sandwich

Those who love Reuben sandwiches as much as we do don't really care if they were invented by the proprietor of a now defunct Manhattan deli or in Omaha (there's even a school of thought that holds out Atlantic City as the mythical source of origin).

As tempting as it might be to go straight from the pressure cooker to the sandwich board, don't. The sandwich will be better made the next day from leftovers—if you start with well-chilled corned beef, it will be much easier to slice the thin shavings that will make for a superior sandwich. Shave the corned beef thin, but pile it up; these sandwiches should be meals unto themselves. Serve with kosher dills on the side.

MAKES 2 SANDWICHES

2 tablespoons Russian dressing

4 slices pumpernickel or dark rye bread

6 to 8 ounces very thinly sliced cooked Classic Corned Beef (opposite)

½ cup sauerkraut, washed and drained

2 large slices Swiss cheese

Spread the Russian dressing over 2 slices of the bread. Divide the corned beef between the 2 slices. Top each with ¼ cup of the sauerkraut and a slice of cheese, making sure the slices are large enough to drape over the other ingredients. Top each with a second slice of bread and flatten slightly. Grill in a dry skillet over medium heat or broil until the cheese has melted and the bread is lightly toasted, 2 to 3 minutes per side.

ELECTRIC
COMPATIBLE
with Revision:

*Cook at high pressure for
29 minutes if you have a
model that works only at
high pressure.*

Texas Chili Beef Ribs

**These are lip-smacking, finger-lickin' beef ribs in a gooey barbecue
sauce spiked with a mess of chili powder, just like they would serve
them up at your favorite down-home Texas rib joint (which in our
case happens to be Bubba's Barbecue, actually situated up the road a
bit in northwest Arkansas. Wouldn't you just know it was in Arkansas
with a name like Bubba's?) Beef ribs are delectable, but they do tend
to give off a fair amount of fat. Either skim the sauce with a gravy
separator before serving or make a day ahead, refrigerate, and skim
off the congealed fat before reheating.**

MAKES 4 SERVINGS

4 pounds beef ribs, trimmed of visible fat

1 large yellow onion, chopped (about $1\frac{1}{2}$ cups)

4 medium stalks celery, chopped (about $1\frac{1}{3}$ cups)

1 clove garlic, minced

$\frac{1}{2}$ cup ketchup

$\frac{1}{4}$ cup red wine vinegar

2 tablespoons Worcestershire sauce

1 tablespoon Dijon mustard

$\frac{1}{4}$ cup firmly packed dark brown sugar

$1\frac{1}{2}$ tablespoons chili powder

$\frac{1}{2}$ teaspoon salt

$\frac{1}{4}$ teaspoon ground black pepper

Combine the ribs, onion, celery, and garlic in a pressure cooker. Mix
together the ketchup, vinegar, Worcestershire sauce, mustard, and
brown sugar and pour the mixture on top. Sprinkle with the chili powder, salt, and pepper. Cover, lock, and bring to low pressure over high
heat. Adjust the heat to stabilize pressure and cook for 35 minutes.
(Cook for 29 minutes if your cooker works only at high pressure.)

Remove the pressure cooker from the heat and let the pressure
drop naturally. Carefully remove the cover. Remove the ribs to a plate
and cover with foil to keep warm. Pour the remaining contents of the

cooker into a gravy separator to skim the fat or into a measuring cup and spoon the fat from the top.

Meaty Chili

We like to serve this hearty chili, which is something of a cross between soup and stew, on tortilla chips in a bowl. Serve garnishes—such as chopped onion, chopped jalapeño chiles, shredded sharp Cheddar or Monterey Jack cheese, and lime wedges—on the side. This is the perfect party food (How do you spell Super Bowl?) and the recipe is easily doubled or tripled.

ELECTRIC COMPATIBLE
with Revision:

Use the browning setting to brown the meat.

MAKES 6 SERVINGS

$^1\!/_2$ tablespoon olive oil

1 pound beef round, trimmed and cut into $^1\!/_2$-inch cubes

8 ounces pork loin sirloin, trimmed and cut into $^1\!/_2$-inch cubes

2 medium stalks celery, diced (about $^2\!/_3$ cup)

1 medium yellow onion, diced (about 1 cup)

1 medium green bell pepper, diced (about 1 cup)

2 large cloves garlic, minced

1 (14$^1\!/_2$-ounce) can diced tomatoes

$^3\!/_4$ cup dry red wine

$^1\!/_4$ cup chili powder

2 teaspoons masa harina

1 tablespoon dried oregano

1 teaspoon salt

1 bay leaf

$^1\!/_4$ cup chopped fresh cilantro

1 teaspoon grated lime zest

Preheat a pressure cooker over medium-high heat and add the oil. Add the beef and pork and brown the meat all over, 4 to 5 minutes. Add the celery, onion, bell pepper, garlic, tomatoes, and wine. Stir in the chili powder, masa harina, oregano, salt, and bay leaf. Cover, lock, and bring to high pressure over high heat. Reduce the heat to stabilize pressure and cook for 20 minutes.

Remove the pressure cooker from the heat and let the pressure drop naturally. Carefully remove the cover; discard the bay leaf, and stir in the cilantro and lime zest.

Asian Roast Beef

This is wonderfully flavorful and juicy rare roast beef—just how Barry, who has been known to consume about twice his body weight in rare roast beef, likes it. It is a far cry from the falling apart piece of pot roast that first comes to mind when one thinks of a whole beef roast cooked in the pressure cooker. This is what Barry makes for a quick roast beef fix, because it cooks up in but a fraction of the time conventional methods require. Start with a good grade of beef, such as choice or prime, for this recipe and cook for 2 minutes more if you prefer your beef medium-rare.

MAKES 6 SERVINGS

1 (2-pound) sirloin tip beef roast

3 cloves garlic, minced

2 stalks lemon grass, sliced (about 3 tablespoons)

3 green onions, trimmed to white and light green parts and chopped (about 3 tablespoons)

1 tablespoon grated fresh ginger

¼ cup ketchup

¼ cup reduced-sodium soy sauce

2 tablespoons sherry

1 tablespoon honey

Put the beef roast into a pressure cooker. Mix together the remaining ingredients and pour the mixture over the roast. Cover, lock, and bring

ELECTRIC COMPATIBLE
with Revision:

If the pressure has not lowered naturally after 15 minutes, use the quick-release button. Use the browning setting to reduce the liquid.

to high pressure over high heat. Reduce the heat to stabilize pressure and cook for 16 minutes.

Remove the pressure cooker from the heat and let the pressure drop naturally. Carefully remove the cover. Remove the roast beef and cover it with foil to keep warm until ready to slice. Bring the liquid in the cooker to a rapid boil and boil until reduced by half, to about ¾ cup, 4 to 5 minutes. Drizzle about 2 tablespoons of the gravy over each serving.

German Pot Roast

For our take on the traditional long-cooking "sour roast" or sauer-braten, we dispense with the usual long marinade and make a couple of ingredient updates, substituting balsamic vinegar for the usual cider vinegar to add a touch more sweetness and replacing sweet paprika with hot for added spice. Look for the dried spaetzle—much quicker to prepare than the homemade fresh variety—in better supermarkets or specialty stores; we buy it from our German butcher.

ELECTRIC
COMPATIBLE
with Revision:

If your cooker is a model that can be set to cook for only 30 minutes, reprogram it for an additional 30 minutes after the roast has cooked for 30 minutes. Then reprogram it for another 15 minutes. Use the browning setting to heat the spaetzle and sauce.

MAKES 6 SERVINGS

½ cup balsamic vinegar

½ cup defatted Beef Stock (page 41 or canned)

¼ cup firmly packed light brown sugar

½ tablespoon hot paprika

1 teaspoon caraway seeds

1 (3-pound) beef rump roast

12 ounces dried German spaetzle

½ cup heavy cream

Combine the vinegar, stock, brown sugar, paprika, and caraway seeds in a pressure cooker. Stir to mix. Add the roast and turn it in the sauce to coat. Cover, lock, and bring to high pressure over high heat. Reduce the heat to stabilize pressure and cook for 75 minutes.

Remove the pressure cooker from the heat and let the pressure

drop naturally. Carefully remove the cover, transfer the roast to a cutting board, and cover it with foil to keep warm.

Meanwhile, bring a large pot of water to a boil, add the spaetzle and boil until al dente, about 20 minutes. Drain. Whisk the cream into the liquid in the pressure cooker, add the spaetzle and cook over medium heat until the sauce has thickened and the noodles have plumped, about 5 minutes. Spoon spaetzle and sauce onto dinner plates. Slice the meat and serve alongside the spaetzle.

Beef Shanks with Figs

An inexpensive cut of meat becomes scrumptious fare fit for company with this recipe. Beef shanks have been our favorite Sunday evening food for years, although they used to take us quite a bit longer to prepare. In addition to reducing the cooking time to a fraction of that required to prepare shanks in the conventional manner, we've found that pressure cooking does a better job of tenderizing the meat as well.

This dish is particularly well suited to preparation the day before serving. Simply let the contents of the cooker cool to room temperature, transfer to an airtight container, and refrigerate. The next day, skim off fat that has risen and congealed before reheating the shanks on the stovetop or in a microwave oven.

MAKES 4 SERVINGS

2 tablespoons vegetable oil

¼ cup all-purpose flour

½ teaspoon salt

¼ teaspoon ground black pepper

1 teaspoon paprika

4 (8-ounce) beef shanks

1 medium white onion, chopped (about 1 cup)

1 large carrot, peeled and chopped (about ½ cup)

2 small stalks celery, chopped (about ½ cup)

ELECTRIC
COMPATIBLE
with Revision:

If your cooker is a model that can be set to cook for only 30 minutes, cook the dish for only 30 minutes.

2 teaspoons dried basil

$\frac{1}{2}$ tablespoon dried thyme or 1 tablespoon fresh thyme

2 teaspoons minced garlic

$\frac{1}{2}$ cup defatted Chicken Stock (page 36 or canned)

$\frac{1}{2}$ cup dry red wine

2 plum tomatoes, seeded and chopped (about $\frac{2}{3}$ cup)

12 dried Mission figs, stemmed and halved

Heat the oil in a pressure cooker over medium-high heat. Meanwhile, mix the flour with the salt, pepper, and paprika and dust the shanks with the mixture. Brown the beef shanks on both sides in the oil, 5 to 6 minutes, and remove them to a plate.

To the cooker, add the onion, carrot, celery, basil, thyme, and garlic. Sauté until the vegetables are tender, about 10 minutes. Add the stock, wine, and tomatoes, stirring to dislodge any browned bits stuck to the bottom of the cooker. Return the shanks to the cooker and add the figs. Cover, lock, and bring to high pressure over high heat. Reduce the heat to stabilize pressure and cook for 35 minutes.

Remove the pressure cooker from the heat and let the pressure drop naturally. Carefully remove the cover. Transfer the shanks to a serving platter and spoon the sauce over the beef.

Bill's Short Ribs and Cabbage

This recipe comes from our friend William Rice at the *Chicago Tribune*. Bill describes short ribs as "soul-warming," a sentiment with which we heartily agree. They're a perfect cold-weather food and perfectly suited to preparation in the pressure cooker, because this cut of meat needs long, moist cooking to tenderize it. Pressure cooking knocks a good 1$\frac{1}{2}$ hours off the time it takes to make the dish. Browning intensifies the flavor and renders some of the fat as well.

MAKES 4 SERVINGS

ELECTRIC
COMPATIBLE
with Revision:

After removing the ribs from the cooker, cook the vegetables and sauce at high pressure for 6 minutes if your cooker works only at high pressure.

1½ tablespoons olive oil

3 pounds beef short ribs, trimmed of visible fat

½ cup dry red wine

½ cup defatted Beef Stock (page 41 or canned)

½ teaspoon Worcestershire sauce

1 bay leaf

1 teaspoon celery salt

¼ teaspoon crushed red pepper flakes

1 medium yellow onion, chopped (about 1 cup)

1 medium tomato, seeded and chopped (about 1 cup)

1 large or 2 small carrots, peeled and chopped (about ½ cup)

12 ounces green cabbage, cored and shredded (about 4 cups)

3 large cloves garlic, chopped

½ tablespoon paprika

½ tablespoon dried oregano

½ tablespoon red wine vinegar

Preheat a pressure cooker over medium heat and swirl in the oil. Add the short ribs and brown on all sides, 4 to 6 minutes. Remove the ribs to a plate and pour out the drippings from the cooker.

To the cooker, add the wine, stirring to dislodge any browned bits stuck to the bottom. Add the stock, Worcestershire sauce, bay leaf, celery salt, and pepper flakes. Return the ribs to the cooker. Cover, lock, and bring to high pressure over high heat. Reduce the heat to stabilize pressure and cook for 30 minutes.

Lower the pressure by a quick-release method. Carefully open the cover. Remove the ribs to a plate and cover with foil to keep warm. Stir the onion, tomato, carrots, cabbage, garlic, paprika, oregano, and vinegar into the cooker. Re-cover, lock, and bring to low pressure. Adjust the heat to stabilize pressure and cook for 8 minutes. (Cook for 6 minutes if you have a model that only works at high pressure.)

Once again, lower the pressure by a quick-release method. Distribute the ribs among 4 dinner plates and spoon the sauce on top. Discard the bay leaf.

African Beef and Okra Stew

Coconut milk, peanut sauce, and okra all reflect the African origins of this dish, which we love to make for company and serve with white rice on the side and little bowls of peanuts, golden raisins, shredded coconut, and mango chutney for garnishing.

    Instead of grinding peanuts, we use a reduced-fat peanut butter, which serves to thicken as well as flavor the sauce. By first sautéing the okra until well browned, we make it crunchier and less viscous than it would otherwise be. When preparing the dish in a manual pressure cooker, bring to low pressure over medium rather than high heat so as not to burn the coconut milk.

ELECTRIC
COMPATIBLE
with Revision:

Cook at high pressure for 35 minutes if your cooker works only at high pressure; if your cooker can be set to cook for only 30 minutes, reprogram it for an additional 5 minutes. After adding the okra, use the browning setting to simmer the stew.

MAKES 6 SERVINGS

1 medium yellow onion, chopped (about 1 cup)

½ cup coconut milk

¾ cup defatted Beef Stock (page 41 or canned)

2 tablespoons Curry Powder (page 32 or purchased)

2 large plum tomatoes, seeded and chopped (about 1 packed cup)

1 pound beef round stew meat, trimmed and cut into 1½-inch cubes

⅓ cup reduced-fat peanut butter

1 teaspoon olive oil

8 ounces okra, trimmed

Mix together the onion, coconut milk, stock, curry powder, tomatoes, and beef in a pressure cooker. Cover, lock, and bring to low pressure over medium heat. Adjust the heat to stabilize pressure and cook for 45 minutes.

Remove the pressure cooker from the heat and let the pressure

drop naturally. Carefully remove the cover and stir in the peanut butter. Meanwhile, preheat a medium nonstick skillet over high heat. Swirl in the oil, add the okra, and sauté until well browned on all sides, about 4 minutes. Add the okra to the pressure cooker and simmer over medium heat for 5 minutes.

French Beef Stew

ELECTRIC COMPATIBLE
with Revision:

Let the pressure drop naturally. Use the browning setting to cook the sauce.

This cross between boeuf bourguignonne and a Provençal beef stew is good served on broad egg noodles or rice. Use a cabernet sauvignon, Bordeaux, zinfandel, or other full-bodied red wine for the stew. Bear in mind that this is one of those dishes in which the quality of the wine you use will make a difference; don't use a wine in the stew that you wouldn't be happy drinking with it. We have eliminated the flour-and-butter roux with which the stew would normally be started, thickening instead at the end with flour and cooking liquid.

MAKES 6 SERVINGS

2 pounds boneless beef chuck, visible fat removed and cut into 2 × 1-inch pieces

2 large carrots, peeled and cut into 2-inch lengths

2 medium or 1 very large yellow onion, cut into wedges

2 medium tomatoes, peeled, seeded, and chopped (about 1½ cups) or 1 (14½-ounce) can diced tomatoes

2 bay leaves

½ tablespoon chopped fresh rosemary or ½ teaspoon dried rosemary

½ tablespoon chopped fresh thyme or ½ teaspoon dried thyme

¼ teaspoon ground black pepper

1 cup dry red wine

8 ounces white button mushrooms, cleaned, stemmed, and larger mushrooms halved

½ cup pitted kalamata olives

2 tablespoons all-purpose flour

2 small cloves garlic, minced

1 teaspoon finely grated orange zest

2 tablespoons chopped fresh parsley

Combine the beef, carrots, onions, tomatoes, bay leaves, rosemary, thyme, and pepper in a pressure cooker. Add the wine, mushrooms, and olives. Cover, lock, and bring to high pressure over high heat. Reduce the heat to stabilize pressure and cook for 18 minutes.

Lower the heat by a quick-release method. Carefully remove the cover and discard the bay leaves.

In a small bowl, mix together the flour and ½ cup of the cooking liquid from the pressure cooker. Blend and return the mixture to the cooker. Cook the sauce over high heat, stirring occasionally, until thickened, 2 to 3 minutes. Stir in the garlic, orange zest, and parsley.

ELECTRIC
COMPATIBLE
with Revision:

If your cooker is a model that can be set to cook for only 30 minutes, reprogram it for an additional 15 minutes after the roast has cooked for 30 minutes.

Veal Roast

We love lean, delicate veal in almost any form and find a veal roast a nice change from beef roast for entertaining. This simple but elegant rendition, featuring a flavorful pureed vegetable sauce, is ready in less than 1 hour.

MAKES 8 SERVINGS

1 pound fennel, stalks and bulb roughly chopped (about 3¾ cups), feathery ends reserved for garnish

1 large white onion, roughly chopped (about 1¾ cups)

3 medium carrots, peeled and roughly chopped (about 1 cup)

1 (2½- to 3-pound) boneless veal shoulder roast

¼ cup Dijon mustard

1 cup defatted Chicken Stock (page 36 or canned)

1 teaspoon salt

½ teaspoon ground black pepper

Combine the fennel, onion, and carrots in a pressure cooker. Rub the veal roast with the mustard to coat and place it on top of the vegetables. Add the stock. Cover, lock, and bring to high pressure over high heat. Reduce the heat to stabilize pressure and cook for 45 minutes.

Remove the pressure cooker from the heat and let the pressure drop naturally. Carefully remove the cover and transfer the meat to a cutting board. For the sauce, puree the remaining contents of the pan, using a hand-held immersible blender or in a food processor or blender, adding the salt and pepper. Slice the meat and drizzle with the sauce.

Veal Stew

We've put an Italian spin on this straightforward French classic by replacing celery with fennel, the typical Italian pairing of veal and fennel being one of our favorites. Needless to say, the original French version involves several separate browning and reduction steps, whereas the pressure cooker method can do the job all in one pot in less than 20 minutes. We prefer the added richness lent by homemade Brown Chicken Stock, but plain chicken stock or beef stock will do in a pinch.

ELECTRIC
COMPATIBLE
with Revision:

Use the browning setting to sauté the vegetables and brown the meat.

MAKES 6 SERVINGS

$1/2$ cup all-purpose flour

$1/2$ teaspoon salt

$1/2$ teaspoon ground black pepper

2 pounds boneless veal shoulder stew meat, trimmed and cut into 2 × 1-inch pieces

2 tablespoons olive oil

1 large white onion, roughly chopped (about $1\frac{1}{2}$ cups)

1 medium fennel bulb, chopped (about 2 cups)

1 cup Brown Chicken Stock (page 37), defatted Chicken Stock (page 36 or canned), or defatted Beef Stock (page 41 or canned)

2 medium tomatoes, peeled, seeded, and chopped (about $1\frac{1}{2}$ cups) or 1 ($14\frac{1}{2}$-ounce) can diced tomatoes

1 cup dry white wine

1 tablespoon fresh thyme or 1 teaspoon dried thyme

1 tablespoon chopped fresh basil or 1 teaspoon dried basil

4 cloves garlic, peeled

Mix the flour, salt, and pepper together in a large, shallow bowl and dredge the veal in the mixture.

Preheat a pressure cooker over medium heat. Add 1 tablespoon of the oil, the onion, and fennel. Cook, stirring constantly, until the onion begins to turn lightly golden, 2 to 3 minutes. Add the veal and cook, stirring, until the meat is no longer pink, about 3 minutes. Add the stock and stir to dislodge any browned bits stuck to the bottom of the pan. Add the tomatoes, wine, thyme, and basil. Press in the garlic. Cover, lock, and bring to high pressure over high heat. Reduce the heat to stabilize pressure and cook for 13 minutes.

Lower the pressure by a quick-release method. Carefully remove the cover. Add additional salt and pepper to taste.

Veal Breast

ELECTRIC
COMPATIBLE:

Too large for a 4- or 5-quart pressure cooker.

This is real Jewish comfort food, just like Barry's Grandma Nigberg used to serve in her Brooklyn restaurant in days long past. Barry still loves veal breast, but it normally takes at least 3 to 4 hours to cook properly and most of the renditions he has been served in recent years, prepared by cooks with more ambition than patience, have bordered on the inedible. With the pressure cooker, you will need neither Luba Nigberg's magic touch nor the patience of a saint to yield a tender, succulent veal breast. Take care not to buy a piece of meat too large to fit into your pressure cooker; a 2¾- to 3-pound veal breast should fit into most 6- and 8-quart cookers.

MAKES 4 SERVINGS

½ tablespoon olive oil

1 (2¾- to 3-pound) veal breast, trimmed

1 medium stalk celery, thinly sliced (about ⅓ cup)

3 garlic cloves, minced

½ cup dry white wine

½ cup defatted Chicken Stock (page 36 or canned)

8 ounces baby-cut carrots

8 ounces cipolline onions, peeled (see Note, below)

1 pound petite new red potatoes, peeled

¾ teaspoon paprika

¼ teaspoon salt

¼ teaspoon ground black pepper

⅛ teaspoon dried thyme or ½ teaspoon fresh thyme

½ tablespoon cornstarch

1 tablespoon water

1 tablespoon chopped fresh parsley

Preheat a pressure cooker over medium-high heat and swirl in the oil. Add the veal breast, bone side up, and cook until browned, about 2 minutes. Turn the breast over and brown it on the other side, about 1 minute. Remove the veal to a plate.

Add the celery and garlic to the cooker and heat for about 15 seconds, until the garlic begins to give off an aroma. Stir in the wine and stir to dislodge any browned bits stuck to the bottom of the cooker. When the wine comes to a boil, about 15 seconds more, add the stock and return the veal breast to the cooker, bone side down. Scatter the carrots, onions, and potatoes around it and sprinkle the paprika, salt, pepper, and thyme over all. Cover, lock, and bring to high pressure over high heat. Reduce the heat to stabilize pressure and cook for 60 minutes.

Remove the pressure cooker from the heat and let the pressure drop naturally or lower the pressure by a quick-release method. Carefully remove the cover. Remove the veal breast to a cutting board, cover with foil to keep warm, and transfer the vegetables to a plate.

In a small bowl, dissolve the cornstarch in the water. Stir the mixture into the liquid in the pressure cooker. Boil, stirring, until clear and thickened, about 1 minute. Cut the breast into 4 servings and transfer to dinner plates. Distribute the vegetables equally, drizzle each serving with about ½ cup of the gravy, and sprinkle with ¾ teaspoon of the parsley.

NOTE

Cipolline onions: These are available in specialty produce markets and some supermarkets, especially those in Italian neighborhoods (the onions were originally from Italy). An equal amount of boiling onions can be substituted.

ELECTRIC
COMPATIBLE
with Revision:

*Use the browning setting to
brown the veal shanks and
sauté the vegetables.*

Osso Buco

Osso buco is one of those dishes that have achieved almost ritual status among devotees. We've been coaxed into many a neighborhood Italian restaurant with the promise of "the world's best" osso buco and have even been served it by a chef at home for a family birthday dinner. It should be melt-in-the-mouth tender, a quality easily achieved in the pressure cooker. (The chef, unfortunately, oven-baked his to accommodate the large number of dinner party guests, yielding a slightly chewy result.)

To keep a veal (or beef) shank from falling apart as it cooks, tightly wrap kitchen twine once around each shank; snip and discard the twine before serving. You could easily substitute ½ tablespoon anchovy paste for the anchovy fillets if you prefer. We like to finish our osso buco with a sprinkling of parsley, garlic, and the zest of a navel orange. For a more traditional gremolata, substitute an equal amount of lemon zest for the orange zest. Serve the osso buco with little demitasse spoons or even shellfish forks, if you have them—your guests will undoubtedly want to retrieve and devour the marrow, an admitted indulgence but a heavenly one.

MAKES 4 SERVINGS

SHANKS

Salt to taste

Ground black pepper to taste

¼ cup all-purpose flour

4 (7-ounce) veal shanks

½ tablespoon olive oil

1 large carrot, peeled and diced (about ½ cup)

1 small yellow onion, diced (about ¾ cup)

2 small stalks celery, diced (about ½ cup)

3 small cloves garlic, minced

2 medium tomatoes, peeled, seeded, and chopped (about 1½ cups) or 1 (14½-ounce) can diced tomatoes

½ cup dry white wine

½ cup defatted Beef Stock (page 41 or canned)

2 anchovy fillets, minced (about $\frac{1}{2}$ tablespoon)

$1\frac{1}{2}$ tablespoons chopped fresh basil

$\frac{1}{2}$ tablespoon fresh thyme or $\frac{1}{2}$ teaspoon dried

GREMOLATA

2 tablespoons chopped fresh parsley

1 tablespoon grated orange zest

4 cloves garlic, minced

Salt, pepper, and flour the veal shanks.

Preheat a pressure cooker over high heat and add the oil. Add the veal shanks and cook until browned on both sides, 5 to 6 minutes. Transfer the shanks to a plate.

Add the carrot, onion, celery, and garlic to the cooker and cook until the onion has just started to color, about 2 minutes. Add the tomatoes, wine, stock, anchovies, basil, and thyme. Bring to a boil and return the shanks to the cooker. Cover, lock, and bring to high pressure over high heat. Reduce the heat to stabilize pressure and cook for 25 minutes.

Meanwhile, make the gremolata by mixing together the parsley, orange zest, and garlic in a small bowl.

Lower the pressure by a quick-release method. Carefully remove the cover. Sprinkle a bit of the gremolata over each serving or pass it on the side.

Veal Kidney Ragoût

We fell in love with the flavor of veal kidney the first time we had it. We were at one of the elaborate New Year's Eve revillon dinners for which Parisian restaurants are rightly famed—sometime after the doors were shut to spare the evening's revelers from interruption and sometime before the requisite band marched through the dining room at the stroke of midnight. Perhaps that festive memory has something

ELECTRIC
COMPATIBLE
with Revision:

Use the browning setting to bring the gravy to a gentle boil.

to do with our positive inklings toward veal kidney, but we would like to think of it as well as simple appreciation of the sweet tender meat James Beard described as delectable.

In our somewhat lighter, and quicker, adaptation of the French classic, we use skim milk instead of heavy cream. Although kidney is high in cholesterol, it is very low in fat and a stellar source of vitamin A and iron. Serve the ragoût with rice, noodles, or even gnocchi.

MAKES 4 SERVINGS

12 ounces veal kidney, fatty cores removed, and sliced

1 large yellow onion, chopped (about 1½ cups)

1 large green bell pepper, chopped (about 1½ cups)

4 ounces white button mushrooms, cleaned, stemmed, and quartered

¼ cup Madeira

¼ cup defatted Chicken Stock (page 36 or canned)

3 sprigs fresh thyme

1 bay leaf

½ teaspoon salt

¼ teaspoon ground black pepper

2 tablespoons instant flour

¼ cup skim milk

2 tablespoons chopped fresh parsley

Combine the veal kidney, onion, bell pepper, mushrooms, wine, stock, thyme, bay leaf, salt, and pepper in a pressure cooker. Cover, lock, and bring to high pressure over high heat. Reduce the heat to stabilize pressure and cook for 10 minutes.

Remove the pressure cooker from the heat and let the pressure drop naturally. Carefully remove the cover. Remove and discard the thyme and bay leaf. Mix the flour and milk together in a small bowl; stir the mixture into the cooker. Bring to a boil over high heat and boil, stirring, until thickened, about 2 minutes. Stir in the parsley.

Tangy Tongue

One of Kevin's favorite destinations is camouflaged behind a nonde-script storefront on a commercial strip in Chicago that is vibrant with signs of Latin street life. Moving through a neat-as-a-pin grocery store, you proceed on past a meat market (hence the establishment's name, Carniceria Leon), into a tiny but bustling tacqueria that serves up, in Kevin's humble opinion, just about the best tongue burritos in the world.

Tongue is one of those inexpensive, long-cooking cuts of meat turned into a succulent, tender treat by pressure cooking. Long popu-lar in many cultures, it can be served simply sliced (or in a sandwich) with mustard, as well as in more elaborate preparations such as Kevin's burrito.

ELECTRIC
COMPATIBLE
with Revision:

If your cooker is a model that can be set to cook for only 30 minutes, reprogram it for an additional 25 minutes after the tongue has cooked for 30 minutes.

MAKE 6 TO 8 SERVINGS

1 (3- to 3½-pound) fresh beef tongue

1 large stalk celery, trimmed and halved

1 large carrot, trimmed (but not peeled) and halved

1 medium yellow onion, peeled

2 cloves garlic, peeled

1 bay leaf

½ teaspoon pickling spice

2 teaspoons salt

5 cups water

Combine all ingredients in a pressure cooker. Cover, lock, and bring to high pressure over high heat. Reduce the heat to stabilize pressure and cook for 55 minutes.

Remove the pressure cooker from the heat and let the pressure drop naturally. Carefully remove the cover, remove the tongue to a plate, and discard the remaining contents of the cooker. Let the tongue cool, then peel it, cut off the root end, and thinly slice.

ELECTRIC
COMPATIBLE
with Revision:

*If your cooker is a model
that can be set to cook for
only 30 minutes, reprogram
it for an additional 10
minutes after the stew has
cooked for 30 minutes.*

Oxtail Stew

**Food and wine columnist William Rice has said that the world is
divided into two kinds of folks—those who eat gelatin (i.e., the gelati-
nous so-called specialty meats such as oxtail and tongue) and those
who do not. While perhaps members of a strident culinary minority,
we enthusiastically declare ourselves firmly in the former camp. Bill
writes about "oxtail's extraordinary meaty flavor and firm texture, plus
its intense richness," a judgment with which we thoroughly concur.
We usually make the stew a night ahead, refrigerate the oxtails and
the sauce separately, and then skim the congealed fat before reheating.**

MAKES 4 SERVINGS

½ tablespoon olive oil

2 pounds oxtails

1 large yellow onion, chopped (about 1½ cups)

1 medium stalk celery, chopped (about ⅓ cup)

1 medium carrot, peeled and chopped (about ⅓ cup)

½ cup defatted Chicken Stock (page 36 or canned)

½ cup dry white wine

½ cup tomato sauce

1 tablespoon fresh oregano or 1 teaspoon dried oregano

1 tablespoon fresh thyme or 1 teaspoon dried thyme

½ tablespoon anchovy paste

Preheat a pressure cooker over medium heat and add the oil. Add the
oxtails and cook until browned all over, 12 to 15 minutes.

Remove the meat to a plate and pour off the fat. Add the onion,
celery, and carrot to the pressure cooker. Cook, stirring constantly,
until the onion turns golden, about 1 minute. Add the stock and stir to
dislodge any browned bits stuck to the bottom of the cooker. Add the
remaining ingredients and stir to mix well. Return the oxtails to the
cooker, cover, lock, and bring to high pressure over high heat. Reduce
the heat to stabilize pressure and cook for 40 minutes.

Lower the pressure by a quick-release method. Carefully remove
the cover.

Pistachio Country Pâté

Our lighter and healthier version of a classic pâté keeps the diced ham of the original, but replaces the pork with turkey, replaces the cream with skim milk, and does away with the pork fat entirely. The original version, formed in a long terrine and submerged in a hot water bath, can take up to 2 hours to cook. We form our pâté in mini loaf pans that will fit easily into a pressure cooker and cook them for only 20 minutes at high pressure. For a denser textured pâté weigh each loaf down with a can of beans turned on its side while it sets in the refrigerator. Slice the pâté and serve it with cornichons and grainy mustard.

ELECTRIC
COMPATIBLE
with Revision:

If you can't fit both mini loaf pans into your cooker at once, cook them in batches.

MAKES 10 SERVINGS

4 ounces ham steak, trimmed and diced

1 pound ground turkey

4 ounces turkey tenderloin, diced

3 ounces pistachio nuts, shelled (about $\frac{1}{4}$ cup)

1 teaspoon salt

1 teaspoon dried tarragon

$\frac{1}{2}$ teaspoon ground allspice

$\frac{1}{4}$ teaspoon ground white pepper

$\frac{1}{3}$ cup skim milk

2 tablespoons cognac

3 cups water

Combine all ingredients, except the water, in a large bowl. Mix together well and let sit for 5 minutes.

Divide the mixture between 2 greased 5¾-inch mini loaf pans, lifting and dropping the pans on a work surface so that the contents settle with no air pockets. Wrap the pans tightly with foil. Put a trivet or a small wire rack into a pressure cooker. Add the water and place the loaf pans on the trivet. Cover, lock, and bring to high pressure over high heat. Reduce the heat to stabilize pressure and cook for 20 minutes.

Remove the pressure cooker from the heat and let the pressure

drop naturally. Carefully remove the cover. Cover and chill the loaves for 3 to 4 hours or overnight in the refrigerator.

VARIATIONS

Pork Pâté: Replace the ground turkey with an equal amount of ground pork, omit the diced turkey tenderloin, double the amount of diced ham called for, and substitute heavy cream for the skim milk.

Veal Pâté: Replace the ground turkey with an equal amount of ground veal, replace the diced turkey tenderloin and the diced ham with 8 ounces diced calf's liver, substitute heavy cream for the skim milk, substitute dried thyme for the tarragon, and omit the pistachios.

Choucroute Garni

ELECTRIC
COMPATIBLE
with Revision:

*Use the browning setting
for the initial sautéing and
cooking steps.*

When the chilly winter winds blowing off Lake Michigan prove to be just too much to take without a little added sustenance, we head straight for Jean Joho's Brasserie Jo for a warming Alsatian specialty such as choucroute.

Choucroute, which means "sauerkraut" in French, is a hearty bistro dish composed of sauerkraut cooked with any of a variety of meats, white wine, caraway seeds and/or juniper berries. (Let's not even talk about the goose fat used in the most authentic versions.) We use smoked turkey sausage in our choucroute, but you could substitute the garlic-flavored French Toulouse sausage if some extra fat grams are not a worry at the moment. Buy refrigerated sauerkraut in plastic bags, which is considerably fresher tasting than the jarred or canned version.

MAKES 4 SERVINGS

> ½ tablespoon olive oil
>
> 1 large yellow onion, sliced (about 1¾ cups)
>
> 2 pounds sauerkraut, rinsed and drained
>
> ½ tablespoon caraway seeds

1 teaspoon dried sage

¼ teaspoon ground black pepper

8 ounces smoked turkey sausage, cut into 16 pieces

4 thin-cut (6-ounce-each) loin center pork chops, visible fat removed

2 (12-ounce) baking potatoes, peeled and cut into 6 pieces each

2 bay leaves

1 large clove garlic, minced

1 cup dry white wine

2 tablespoons cider vinegar

Preheat a pressure cooker over high heat and swirl in the oil. Add the onion and sauté until beginning to turn golden, about 1 minute. Add half of the sauerkraut (about 2 cups), the caraway seeds, sage, and pepper. Stir to mix and scatter half of the sausage on top. Add the pork chops in a single layer. Add the remaining sausage and sauerkraut, then the potatoes and bay leaves. Scatter the garlic and pour in the wine and vinegar. Close, lock, and bring to high pressure over high heat. Reduce the heat to stabilize pressure and cook for 9 minutes.

Lower the pressure by a quick-release method. Carefully remove the cover. On each of four dinner plates, place a pork chop and 3 pieces of potato. Remove and discard the bay leaves. Stir the rest of the contents of the cooker together and divide the mixture among the 4 plates.

Smothered Rabbit

Our update of an old-time Midwestern recipe, this dish features lean rabbit smothered in a rich gravy made from the cooking liquid. We add a few dashes of bitters to lend the gravy an interesting accent, along with Spanish olives and mushrooms. Rabbit is particularly good when prepared by a moist cooking method, such as braising or pressure cooking, which takes a fraction of the time of the original

ELECTRIC
COMPATIBLE

method. Frozen, cut-up rabbit has become increasingly available of late; fresh rabbit is often available from a butcher.

MAKES 4 SERVINGS

$\frac{1}{4}$ cup all-purpose flour

$\frac{1}{2}$ teaspoon salt

$\frac{1}{4}$ teaspoon ground black pepper

1 ($2\frac{3}{4}$- to 3-pound) young rabbit, cut up

2 tablespoons olive oil

1 medium yellow onion, sliced (about 1 cup)

2 medium carrots, peeled and sliced (about $\frac{2}{3}$ cup)

2 medium stalks celery, sliced (about $\frac{2}{3}$ cup)

$1\frac{1}{2}$ cups defatted Chicken Stock (page 36 or canned)

$\frac{1}{2}$ tablespoon Angostura bitters

4 ounces white button mushrooms, cleaned, stemmed, and thinly sliced (about 1 cup)

6 pimiento-stuffed Spanish olives, thinly sliced (about 3 tablespoons)

Combine the flour, salt, and pepper in a plastic bag. In batches, shake the rabbit in the mixture to coat.

Preheat a large nonstick skillet over medium heat and swirl in the oil. Add the rabbit in a single layer and cook until browned on both sides, 12 to 15 minutes. Transfer the rabbit to a pressure cooker. To the skillet, add the onion, carrots, and celery. Cook, stirring occasionally, until the onion has just begun to brown lightly, about 3 minutes. Transfer the vegetables to the pressure cooker.

Add the stock and bitters to the skillet. Increase the heat to high, bring to a simmer, and stir to dislodge any browned bits stuck to the bottom of the pan, about $1\frac{1}{2}$ minutes. Pour over the rabbit and vegetables in the cooker. Cover, lock, and bring to high pressure over high heat. Reduce the heat to stabilize pressure and cook for 30 minutes.

Lower the pressure by a quick-release method. Carefully remove the cover. Stir in the mushrooms and olives. Re-cover (but do not lock) the cooker and let sit off heat for 5 minutes to allow the mushrooms to cook.

Spring Lamb Stew

In this recipe, we perk up traditional lamb stew with a bit of pungent hot paprika. Use tender spring lamb, which is usually from lambs 3 to 5 months of age, if you can find it. (Regular lamb is from sheep 6 months to 1 year old.) The pinker the lamb, the younger and better quality it is, the darker the more advanced toward mutton. For this dish, choose a leaner leg cut of lamb and cube it rather than buying prepared stew meat, which is typically from the shoulder. Serve the stew with crusty bread.

ELECTRIC
COMPATIBLE
with Revision:

Compatible only if your cooker works at low pressure. Use the browning setting to brown the meat.

MAKES 6 SERVINGS

1 tablespoon all-purpose flour

1 teaspoon hot paprika

$^{1}/_{2}$ teaspoon salt

1 pound boneless lamb leg stew meat, trimmed and cut into 1-inch cubes

2 teaspoons olive oil

1 cup defatted Chicken Stock (page 36 or canned)

8 ounces cipolline onions, peeled (see Note, page 61)

8 ounces baby-cut carrots

6 ounces peas (about 1 cup), fresh or frozen and thawed

12 ounces (12 to 14) petite new red potatoes, scrubbed and halved

2 tablespoons chopped fresh rosemary

Combine the flour, paprika, and salt in a large, shallow bowl. Toss the lamb in the mixture to coat.

Preheat a pressure cooker over medium heat and add the oil. Add the lamb and cook, stirring constantly, until well-browned, about 2 minutes. Add the stock and stir to dislodge browned bits stuck to the bottom of the cooker. Add the vegetables and the rosemary. Cover, lock, and bring to low pressure over high heat. Reduce the heat to maintain pressure and cook for 12 minutes.

Lower the pressure by a quick-release method. Carefully remove the cover. Let sit for 5 minutes before serving.

Lamb Shanks with Rosemary and Green Olives

ELECTRIC
COMPATIBLE
with Revision:

Use the browning setting for the initial browning and cooking steps.

This dish, with its combination of lamb and olives, is very Italian in feel. We even finish it with an orange zest, parsley, and garlic mixture reminiscent of the gremolata containing lemon zest that Italians sprinkle over veal shanks for osso buco. Choose any large, plump Mediterranean olives packed in brine. To pit the olives easily, first crack the flesh by smashing them with a wooden spoon or the flat side of a large knife.

Even shank, one of the leanest cuts of lamb, will come out of the pressure cooker juicy, because this moist cooking method doesn't require the marbleization of fattier cuts to tenderize. We usually cook the shanks the night before, refrigerate overnight so that any fat will rise for easy skimming, and then re-warm over medium heat for about 15 minutes before serving.

MAKES 4 SERVINGS

$\frac{1}{2}$ tablespoon olive oil

4 (12-ounce) lamb shanks

1 medium yellow onion, chopped (about 1 cup)

4 cloves garlic, chopped

1 (14$\frac{1}{2}$-ounce) can diced tomatoes

$\frac{1}{2}$ cup dry white wine

2 teaspoons chopped fresh rosemary or 1 teaspoon dried rosemay

1 teaspoon fennel seeds

Ground black pepper to taste

½ cup chopped green olives in brine

1 tablespoon grated orange zest

2 tablespoons chopped fresh parsley

Preheat a pressure cooker over medium heat and swirl in the oil. Add the lamb shanks and cook until lightly browned on both sides, 3 to 5 minutes. Add the onion and 3 cloves of the garlic. Cook, stirring constantly, until the onion begins to turn golden, 2 to 3 minutes. Add the tomatoes, wine, rosemary, fennel seeds, and pepper. Cover, lock, and bring to high pressure over high heat. Reduce the heat to stabilize pressure and cook for 25 minutes.

Lower the pressure by a quick-release method. Carefully remove the cover. Stir in the olives and set aside for 5 to 10 minutes. Meanwhile, mix together the orange zest, parsley, and the remaining garlic clove in a small bowl. Stir in the mixture before serving.

Moroccan Lamb and Prune Tagine

 ELECTRIC
COMPATIBLE

We have long loved the sweet-savory taste of *tagines*, Moroccan slow-cooked stews made with meat and dried fruit, and long admired the work of Paula Wolfert, the doyenne of Moroccan cooking. Paula, an early advocate of pressure cookery, notes that it is the pressure cooker that has allowed residents in many parts of the Mediterranean basin to continue to prepare their traditional long-cooking dishes on weekdays, given the changing nature of the work world and of Mediterranean women's place in it.

Precut lamb stew meat usually comes from the shoulder. If you prefer, use a leaner leg or shank cut that has been trimmed and cubed. This dish, thickened as well as flavored by the prunes, uses such typically Middle Eastern seasonings as cumin and coriander; we have added a novel twist by substituting cilantro for parsley. Serve the tagine with couscous.

MAKES 6 SERVINGS

1½ pounds lamb stew meat, trimmed and cut into 1-inch cubes

8 ounces boiling onions, peeled

1 cup pitted prunes

2 (2 × 1-inch) pieces fresh ginger

4 cloves garlic, minced

1 cinnamon stick

1 teaspoon ground cumin

½ teaspoon ground coriander

½ teaspoon salt

½ teaspoon ground black pepper

½ cup defatted Beef Stock (page 41 or canned)

2 teaspoons grated lemon zest

2 tablespoons chopped cilantro

Combine the lamb, onions, prunes, ginger, garlic, cinnamon, cumin, coriander, salt, pepper, and stock in a pressure cooker. Cover, lock, and bring to high pressure over high heat. Reduce the heat to stabilize pressure and cook for 15 minutes.

Lower the pressure by a quick-release method. Carefully remove the cover. Remove and discard the cinnamon stick and ginger. Stir in the lemon zest and cilantro.

Russian Lamb and Artichokes

ELECTRIC
COMPATIBLE

This is our updated version of a classic Georgian dish incorporating lamb, artichokes, and hot chile pepper. We've added sunchokes, one of our favorite vegetables, and some seasoning variations that make for a unique and satisfying meal. For a milder dish, use the chile pepper whole and discard it before serving; if you like things a bit hotter, core, seed, devein, and chop the chile and add it to the dish.

Also called Jerusalem artichokes, nutritious sunchokes have nothing to do with Israeli cooking and are actually native to North America. They taste like a cross between a globe artichoke heart and a sweeter version of a white potato. In addition to lending flavor, they fall apart and thicken this dish, creating a very rich sauce.

MAKES 4 SERVINGS

$1\frac{1}{2}$ pounds lamb stew meat (shoulder, shank, or leg), trimmed and cut into $\frac{1}{2}$-inch cubes

1 (9-ounce) box frozen artichoke hearts, thawed

6 ounces sunchokes, peeled and quartered (about $\frac{3}{4}$ cup)

1 red finger chile pepper, whole or cored, seeded, deveined, and chopped (see headnote)

$\frac{1}{2}$ cup tomato sauce

$\frac{1}{4}$ cup dry red wine

$\frac{1}{2}$ tablespoon dried oregano

$\frac{1}{2}$ teaspoon salt

$\frac{1}{2}$ teaspoon sugar

2 tablespoons chopped fresh parsley

Grated zest of 1 lemon

1 clove garlic, minced

Combine the lamb, artichoke hearts, sunchokes, chile pepper, tomato sauce, wine, oregano, salt, and sugar in a pressure cooker. Cover, lock, and bring to high pressure over high heat. Reduce the heat to stabilize pressure and cook for 10 minutes.

Lower the pressure by a quick-release method. Carefully remove the cover. Stir in the parsley, lemon zest, and garlic and serve.

ELECTRIC
COMPATIBLE

Apple Pork Loin

Pork with tart green apple is a traditional flavor combination that shows up in the cuisine of many European cultures. In this dish, the taste is boosted by the addition of Calvados, the classic apple brandy of Normandy; you could substitute any similar tasting liqueur, such as sour apple schnapps. Although most of the European renditions would incorporate paprika, we like the additional flavor boost of cayenne and paprika contained in American Creole seasoning.

Be sure not to confuse pork loin roast with very thin and much faster cooking pork tenderloin, which will not work in this recipe. We have timed the recipe so that the pork will be cooked to about medium-rare (medium in an electric cooker, which takes longer for the pressure to release naturally); if you prefer your pork closer to well done, cook for 2 minutes more.

The consistency of the puree can vary greatly, depending on the moisture content of the apple. It should be the consistency of soft applesauce; if it is too thin initially, strain out the excess liquid to achieve a thicker consistency.

MAKES 6 SERVINGS

1 large yellow onion, cut into 1-inch chunks (about 1 1/2 cups)

1 Granny Smith apple, peeled and cut into 1-inch chunks (about 1 1/4 cups)

1 acorn squash, peeled, seeded, and cut into 1-inch chunks (about 1 1/2 cups)

1/4 cup Calvados

1/4 cup defatted Chicken Stock (page 36 or canned)

2 cloves garlic, minced

1/2 teaspoon salt

1/4 teaspoon ground black pepper

1 tablespoon Creole Seasoning (see below)

1 (2-pound) boneless pork loin roast

Put the onion, apple, and squash into a pressure cooker. Add the Calvados, stock, garlic, salt, and pepper and mix well. Rub the Creole seasoning all over the pork roast to coat and place the roast on top of the vegetable mixture. Cover, lock, and bring to high pressure over high heat. Reduce the heat to stabilize pressure and cook for 20 minutes.

Remove the pressure cooker from the heat and let the pressure drop naturally. Carefully remove the cover. Remove the pork roast, wrap it in foil, and set aside for 10 minutes.

Meanwhile, whisk the apple and vegetable mixture to create a puree. Slice the pork thinly and serve with the puree.

Creole Seasoning

Try this instead of a commercially prepared Creole seasoning mix.

MAKES ABOUT 7 TABLESPOONS

2 tablespoons ground black pepper

1 tablespoon plus 1 teaspoon dried thyme

1 tablespoon plus 1 teaspoon paprika

1 tablespoon plus 1 teaspoon cayenne pepper

1 tablespoon plus 1 teaspoon coarse salt

Mix all ingredients together. Store in an airtight container for up to 6 months.

Braised Pork in White Wine

ELECTRIC
COMPATIBLE
with Revision:

The Boston butt cut of pork comes from the shoulder as does the cheaper, albeit fattier, picnic cut, sometimes called a picnic ham, which can be substituted in this recipe. The meat may or may not have a thin layer of fat on one side. If so, you can skip the oil unless needed to keep the roast from sticking while browning. This, by the way, is our adaptation of a delicious but somewhat laborious Parisian ham in aspic. We use similar flavorings, but instead of making the cooking liquid into aspic by adding gelatin, we puree it to make a sauce.

If your cooker is a model that can be set to cook for only 30 minutes, reprogram it for an additional 10 minutes after the roast has cooked for 30 minutes. Lower the pressure using the quick-release button.

1 (3-pound) bone-in pork Boston butt roast

½ tablespoon olive oil, or as needed

2 medium carrots, peeled and roughly chopped (about ¾ cup)

9 ounces leek, trimmed to white and light green parts, sliced (about 1 cup), and rinsed well

3 small stalks celery, roughly chopped (about ½ cup)

3 cloves garlic, chopped

2 cups Chardonnay or other dry white wine

1 teaspoon dried thyme or 1 tablespoon fresh thyme

½ teaspoon ground black pepper

Preheat a pressure cooker over medium heat. If the pork roast has a thin layer of fat on one side, place it, fat side down, into the cooker. (If not, first swirl ½ tablespoon oil into the cooker.) Cook until browned, about 3 minutes, turn the roast over and brown on the other side, 2 to 3 minutes, adding oil if needed to prevent sticking.

Remove the roast to a plate and add the carrots, leek, and celery to the cooker. Cook, stirring, until the leek becomes limp, 1 minute. Add the garlic and cook, still stirring, until it is fragrant, about 30 seconds. Add the wine and stir to dislodge any browned bits from the bottom of the cooker. Return the roast to the cooker and sprinkle with the thyme and pepper. Cover, lock, and bring to high pressure over high heat. Reduce the heat to stabilize pressure and cook for 40 minutes.

Remove the pressure cooker from the heat and let the pressure drop naturally. Carefully remove the cover. Remove the roast to a cutting board and slice it. Puree the remaining contents of the cooker for a sauce using a hand-held immersible blender or in a food processor or blender.

Bourbon Pork Roast

We love the rich, woody accent bourbon lends to glazes and gravies. The inspiration for this recipe was actually a bourbon-and-mustard-glazed ham. Here, we take things a step further and make a thick, rich gravy for the pork roast by adding sour cream to the residual cooking liquid. Take care not to boil the gravy vigorously, which would cause the sour cream to break up.

This recipe yields pork cooked to about medium-rare in a stovetop pressure cooker and medium in an electric model; cook for 1 or 2 minutes more if you prefer.

ELECTRIC COMPATIBLE
with Revision:

Use the browning setting to brown the roast and to warm the gravy.

MAKES 4 SERVINGS

$\frac{1}{2}$ tablespoon olive oil

1 (1$\frac{1}{2}$-pound) boneless pork loin roast

$\frac{1}{3}$ cup dry white wine

2 tablespoons packed light brown sugar

1 tablespoon coarse Dijon mustard

6 ounces boiling onions, peeled

6 ounces baby-cut carrots

2 large stalks celery, cut into 1-inch chunks

$\frac{1}{3}$ cup bourbon

$\frac{1}{2}$ teaspoon salt

$\frac{1}{4}$ teaspoon ground black pepper

$\frac{1}{4}$ cup reduced-fat sour cream

2 tablespoons chopped fresh parsley

1 teaspoon snipped fresh chives

Preheat a pressure cooker over medium-high heat and add the oil. Add the roast and cook until browned on both sides, about 1 minute per side. Remove the roast to a plate and add the wine to the cooker and stir to dislodge any browned bits stuck to the bottom of the cooker.

In a small bowl, whisk together the brown sugar and mustard.

Pour the mixture over the roast and return it to the cooker. Scatter the onions, carrots, and celery around the roast. Pour the bourbon over all and sprinkle with the salt and pepper. Cover, lock, and bring to high pressure over high heat. Reduce the heat to stabilize pressure and cook for 15 minutes.

Remove the pressure cooker from the heat and let the pressure drop naturally. Carefully remove the cover. Remove the roast and vegetables and cover them with foil to keep warm. Let the roast sit for about 10 minutes before slicing.

Meanwhile, return the cooker to medium heat and add the sour cream, parsley, and chives to the cooking liquid. Cook until the gravy is steaming and beginning to bubble, about 3 minutes; drizzle about ¼ cup over each serving.

ELECTRIC
COMPATIBLE
with Revision:

Use the browning setting to bring the barbecue sauce to a gentle boil.

Carolina Barbecue Pork

We spend a lot of time on the Outer Banks of North Carolina, mostly for the pleasure of the company of friends with a home there; the natural beauty of the environment; and the mild climate, which provides a nice change from our native Chicago. But the food is also more than a little draw, ranging from succulent shellfish of all sorts served in crab shacks on the beach to the mouth-watering Carolina barbecue dished up in such local hangouts as the Pigman.

This recipe is for Carolina-style "pulled" pork barbecue (in contrast to Texas-style sliced barbecued beef brisket). Preparation of this regional delicacy is normally a multistep process that involves cooking the pork in a vinegar-based marinade, shredding it, and then folding it into a barbecue sauce. Here, we do it all at once in a pressure cooker, cooking the meat in a vinegar-based barbecue sauce until it falls apart easily. The barbecue is best the next day, after the flavors have had a chance to meld. Serve on a roll (traditionally a soft hamburger bun, but we prefer heartier kaiser rolls) with coleslaw and extra sauce on the side.

MAKES 8 SERVINGS

1 large yellow onion, chopped (about 1½ cups)

1 (14½-ounce) can diced tomatoes

½ cup dark corn syrup

½ cup firmly packed dark brown sugar

3 tablespoons cider vinegar

2 tablespoons coarse Dijon mustard

1 tablespoon Worcestershire sauce

¾ teaspoon celery salt

1¼ teaspoons ground black pepper

4 cloves garlic, minced or peeled

1 (3-pound) pork shoulder roast, trimmed and cut into strips, bone reserved

2 tablespoons tomato paste

2 tablespoons pure maple syrup

½ teaspoon mesquite-flavored Liquid Smoke

Combine the onion, tomatoes, corn syrup, brown sugar, vinegar, mustard, Worcestershire sauce, celery salt, and ¾ teaspoon of the pepper in a pressure cooker. Stir in minced garlic or press in whole cloves. Add the strips of pork and the reserved bone. Cover, lock, and bring to high pressure over high heat. Reduce the heat to stabilize pressure and cook for 25 minutes.

Remove the pressure cooker from the heat and let the pressure drop naturally. Carefully remove the cover. Discard the bone and break up the meat with a potato masher or whisk. Mix in the tomato paste, maple syrup, Liquid Smoke, and the remaining ½ teaspoon pepper. Bring the barbecue sauce to a boil over medium-high heat and boil for 10 minutes to thicken.

*Use the browning setting to
bring the sauce to a gentle
boil.*

Barbecue Spareribs

Kevin has been in love with spareribs ever since he first tried them at a neighborhood joint in Chicago's Hyde Park called the Tropical Hut, a very 1950s kind of place all done up in bamboo and rattan and given to serving drinks with little umbrellas stuck in them. But they did have good ribs, drenched in a thick, zesty barbecue sauce of which ours is somewhat reminiscent. Be sure to save any leftover sauce, which freezes well and works nicely with a variety of meats (see Variation); it is a universal sauce in the K.C. style (think Arthur Bryant's of Kansas City, not Sonny Bryan's Dallas smokehouse).

Pressure cooking yields especially moist and juicy spareribs. Although we don't usually consider it necessary to brown meat before pressure cooking, we do so here to add the traditional look of ribs cooked on the grill. You could also achieve the grilled look by skipping the browning step and broiling the ribs for about 2 minutes per side after they come out of the pressure cooker, which is what you should do if you wish to make them a day in advance.

MAKES 4 SERVINGS

1/2 tablespoon vegetable oil

3 to 3 1/2 pounds pork spareribs, cut into 2- or 3-rib pieces

1 large white onion, chopped (about 1 1/2 cups)

4 large cloves garlic, minced

3/4 cup ketchup

1/2 cup cider vinegar

1/3 cup dark molasses

2 tablespoons Dijon mustard

2 tablespoons Worcestershire sauce

1/3 cup firmly packed light brown sugar

1 teaspoon ground black pepper

Preheat a large nonstick skillet over medium-high heat and swirl in the oil. Add the ribs and cook until browned on both sides, 3 to 4 minutes per side, adding a little more oil if the ribs are sticking. Transfer the browned ribs to a pressure cooker.

Combine the remaining ingredients in a bowl. Add the mixture to the cooker. Turn the ribs to coat them in the sauce. Cover, lock, and bring to high pressure over high heat. Reduce the heat to stabilize pressure and cook for 25 minutes.

Lower the pressure by a quick-release method. Carefully remove the cover. Remove the ribs. Bring the sauce to a boil over high heat and boil for about 3 minutes to thicken. Serve the sauce on the side.

VARIATION

Barbecue Chicken: We also like to cook chicken in the same sauce as prepared for our Barbecue Spareribs and will sometimes cook up a platter of each for casual entertaining. You should have enough sauce left over from preparing the ribs to pressure cook a batch of either 4 chicken breasts (bone-in, with skin) or 8 thighs. Brown the chicken before boiling down the sauce to thicken it, as directed in the last step of the recipe. Add the chicken to the sauce in the cooker and cook breasts for 12 minutes on low pressure or 9 minutes on high, thighs for 10 minutes on low or 8 minutes on high.

Poultry

We weren't surprised, when we started testing poultry recipes in the pressure cooker, to find that it produced a mean rendition of homey Chicken with Chive Dumplings in 18 minutes or superb Turkey and Rice–Stuffed Peppers in 12 minutes.

The results of our trials with whole birds and whole turkey breast, on the other hand, were a revelation! We found that not only can the pressure cooker yield some of the best chicken that can be had in a total preparation time of about 25 minutes, but that using it is also the essential first step in preparing succulent duck in 45 minutes without the usual ration of grease and mess. With whole Roasted Duck as with whole Lemon Garlic Chicken, the trick is to partially cook it in a pressure cooker, during which time the fat will be rendered with no spattering, then pop the bird into a hot oven to finish cooking, browning, and crisping.

We use the same pressure cooker-to-oven sequence to prepare whole turkey breast in about 45 minutes from start to finish. What really impressed us was not the quickness of preparation (although we're not complaining), but the improvement in results yielded by starting with the pressure cooker. Just as it is next to impossible by other methods to cook a duck so that it is neither greasy nor dry and stringy, it is equally rare to find turkey breast that has emerged from the oven still moist and juicy. The latter we finish in either one of two ways—a traditional Roast Turkey with Gravy preparation or a Spicy Turkey Mole.

Other than when cooking whole chicken and turkey and a few other such exceptions, we prefer to prepare poultry at low pressure and to remove skin only after cooking—in particular, we find skinless, boneless breast meat cooked at high pressure to be a bit rubbery. Take care to lower the pressure naturally when so directed. When making Duck Confit, for example, using a quick-release method could send a geyser of fat gushing up through the steam valve.

Duck Confit

Salting duck and then cooking and packing it in its own fat is a very old Gascon means of preservation. The yield from this recipe will keep for up to 6 months in the refrigerator, a rich, wonderful treat to have on hand for the ultimate indulgence, Cassoulet (page 163). Confit usually takes 3 to 4 hours of diligent cooking and can produce some messy splatter; our easy confit is done entirely in the pressure cooker and cooks for only 17 minutes. Don't use high pressure (for this reason, confit cannot be done in electric or manual pressure cookers with only a high setting) and do let the pressure drop naturally.

When you trim the duck, save the fat to cook and pack it in (you may need to augment the duck fat with chicken fat or lard), as well as the wings, backbone, neck, and giblets for Duck Stock (page 39), which freezes well and is another component of Cassoulet.

ELECTRIC
COMPATIBLE

Compatible only if your cooker works at low pressure.

MAKES ABOUT 1½ POUNDS

1 (5- to 6-pound) duck

¼ cup coarse salt

½ teaspoon dried thyme

3 bay leaves, crumbled

2½ pounds duck or chicken fat or lard

Place the duck on a cutting board breast side down and make two slits the entire length of the bird, one on each side of the backbone. Remove and reserve the backbone, along with the neck and giblets that will have come packaged with the duck. Butterfly the bird open, turn bone side down, and press down lightly to flatten. Using poultry shears or a sturdy knife, cut the duck in half lengthwise. Cut off and reserve the wings. Cut the legs from the breasts and then cut each leg at the joint between the thigh and drumstick. Remove excess skin and fat from the bird, reserving the fat. Cut each breast in half crosswise.

Mix together the salt, thyme, and bay leaves in a small bowl. Rub the mixture on the duck and place it into a 13 × 9-inch glass dish in a single layer. Cover and refrigerate for 24 hours.

Rinse the salt coating from the duck and pat dry.

You will need 2½ pounds fat; augment the reserved duck fat if necessary with chicken fat or lard. Melt the fat in a pressure cooker over medium heat. Add the duck. Cover, lock, and bring to low pressure over medium heat. Adjust the heat to stabilize pressure and cook for 17 minutes.

Remove the pressure cooker from the heat and let the pressure drop naturally. Carefully remove the cover and allow to cool. Bone the breasts, leaving the skin on. Put the breasts, thighs, and drumsticks into a tight-sealing container and cover with at least a 1-inch layer of fat. Seal and store in the refrigerator for up to 6 months.

Roasted Duck

We'll never prepare duck any other way after trying it from the pressure cooker, which manages to rid the duck of much of its fat without drying it out—the duck emerges even moister than usual—and makes cleanup a snap, because spattering is contained within the cooker. The duck is then popped in the oven for a few minutes to brown.

It's hard to determine portion yields on duck owing to the amount of bones. Figure about 3 servings per duck (we usually prepare 2 ducks in batches to serve 6). A single duck would easily feed 2 hungry diners; methodically carved for maximum yield, it would serve 4 with ample side dishes.

ELECTRIC
COMPATIBLE

Too large for a 4-, 5-, or 6-quart cooker.

MAKES 2 TO 4 SERVINGS

Salt to taste

Ground black pepper to taste

1 (4 1/2- to 5-pound) duck

5 cups water

1 tablespoon unsalted butter at room temperature

Preheat the oven to 475F (245C).

Place a trivet or a small wire rack into a pressure cooker. Salt and pepper the duck inside and out and stand it on the trivet. Add the water. Cover, lock, and bring to high pressure over high heat. Reduce the heat to stabilize pressure and cook for 25 minutes.

Lower the pressure by a quick-release method. Carefully remove the cover. Remove the duck to a roasting pan and rub with the butter. Roast about 20 minutes, until the skin has browned, the juices run clear, and the duck has reached an internal temperature of 170F (75C) on an instant-read thermometer.

Bing Cherry Sauce

An elegant flourish with which to finish duck.

MAKES ABOUT 1 CUP

1 (16½-ounce) can Bing cherries in heavy syrup

2 tablespoons sugar

¼ cup dry red wine

2 tablespoons cornstarch

Put the cherries and their juice into a medium saucepan over medium heat. Stir in the sugar and cook until it has dissolved and the mixture has begun to simmer, about 5 minutes. Remove from the heat. Combine the wine and cornstarch in a small bowl. Stir to dissolve the cornstarch and pour the mixture into the saucepan. Return to the heat and cook over medium heat, stirring constantly, until the sauce has thickened and turned clear, 2 to 3 minutes.

Spicy Turkey Mole

When our friend Patty Oria's mom and aunts prepared turkey mole for Thanksgiving—which they did ritually every Thanksgiving—it was a day-long family project. One sister was in charge of boiling the turkey; the second was in charge of making the basic thick mole; and the third was in charge of ripping turkey meat off the carcass, adding the cook-

ELECTRIC COMPATIBLE

Too large for a 4- or 5-quart pressure cooker.

ing stock to the mole pot, and then cooking the turkey in the mole. The process started early in the morning, and let us just say that everyone had worked up an appetite by the time it was done. Here we condense several steps in the pressure cooker, flavoring the turkey with the mole as it cooks.

MAKES 10 SERVINGS

5 dried ancho chiles (about 3 ounces total)

1 dried New Mexico chile pepper

2$\frac{1}{2}$ cups boiling water

1 (5$\frac{1}{2}$- to 6-pound) fresh turkey breast

1 very large yellow onion, chopped (about 3 cups)

3 plum tomatoes, peeled, seeded, and chopped (about 1$\frac{1}{2}$ cups) or 1 (14$\frac{1}{2}$-ounce) can diced tomatoes

$\frac{1}{4}$ cup golden raisins

1 cinnamon stick

1 bay leaf

6 cloves garlic, peeled

1 tablespoon fresh oregano leaves or 1 teaspoon dried oregano

$\frac{1}{2}$ tablespoon fresh thyme leaves or $\frac{3}{4}$ teaspoon dried thyme

1 tablespoon unsweetened cocoa powder

$\frac{1}{4}$ teaspoon ground allspice

2 tablespoons masa harina

$\frac{1}{4}$ cup plain dry breadcrumbs

$\frac{1}{4}$ cup chopped fresh cilantro

1 tablespoon fresh lime juice

$\frac{1}{4}$ teaspoon grated lime zest

Combine the chiles and boiling water in a bowl, cover, and let steep until the chiles are pliable, about 20 minutes. Stem, core, seed, and devein the chiles. Strain and reserve the soaking liquid.

Combine the turkey breast, onion, tomatoes, raisins, cinnamon stick, and bay leaf in a pressure cooker.

Combine the chiles, garlic, oregano, thyme, cocoa powder, and all-spice in a food processor. Adding the reserved soaking liquid in ½-cup increments, process until smooth. Pour over the turkey breast. Cover, lock, and bring to low pressure over high heat. Reduce the heat to stabilize pressure and cook for 45 minutes.

Lower the pressure by a quick-release method. Carefully remove the cover. Remove the turkey breast to a plate and cover with foil to keep warm. Remove and discard the cinnamon stick and bay leaf. Transfer 1 cup of the cooking liquid to a bowl and mix in the masa harina and breadcrumbs. Return the mixture to the cooker over medium heat. Cook, stirring, until thickened, 1 to 2 minutes; then stir in the cilantro, lime juice, and lime zest. Thinly slice the turkey, arrange on a platter, and pour the mole from the cooker over the meat.

VARIATION

Chicken Mole: We save leftover mole, which freezes well, for cooking chicken breasts. Use a minimum of 1 cup mole for 4 chicken breasts and cook for 12 minutes on low pressure or 9 minutes on high. Or use 8 chicken thighs, cooking for 10 minutes on low pressure or 8 minutes on high.

Turkey and Rice–Stuffed Peppers

Old-fashioned "porcupine meatballs," bursting with rice—a perennial pressure cooker favorite—were the inspiration for this very tasty and filling dish. We stuffed the mixture, here made with low-fat ground turkey rather than beef, into bell peppers and added an international twist or two to bring the recipe up to date. Redolent of cumin and coriander and boasting a turmeric-laced sauce, our modern-day stuffed peppers have a distinctively Indian accent.

MAKES 4 SERVINGS

ELECTRIC
COMPATIBLE

1 pound ground turkey

½ cup long-grain white rice

1 small yellow onion, chopped (about ¾ cup)

1 tablespoon Worcestershire sauce

1 teaspoon ground cumin

¾ teaspoon salt

½ teaspoon ground coriander

¼ teaspoon cayenne pepper

2 very large green bell peppers (about 1½ pounds total), halved lengthwise and cores removed

1 (14½-ounce) can diced tomatoes

1 (8-ounce) can tomato sauce

2 tablespoons chopped fresh cilantro plus extra for garnishing

2 large cloves garlic, chopped

1 teaspoon ground turmeric

Combine the turkey, rice, onion, Worcestershire sauce, cumin, salt, coriander, and cayenne in a large bowl. Mix well. Scoop ⅔ cup of the mixture into the cavity of each bell pepper half.

Combine the tomatoes, tomato sauce, cilantro, garlic, and turmeric in a pressure cooker. Place the stuffed pepper halves on top. Cover, lock, and bring to high pressure over high heat. Reduce the heat to stabilize pressure and cook for 12 minutes.

Lower the pressure by a quick-release method. Carefully remove the cover. Serve each person a stuffed pepper half in a large shallow bowl and spoon about ½ cup of the sauce from the cooker over each serving. Garnish with a sprinkling of cilantro.

Roast Turkey with Gravy

After tasting turkey from the pressure cooker, we may never prepare it any other way. Whereas much turkey meat, especially white meat, is typically very dry, turkey cooked this way comes out of the pressure cooker moist and succulent and is then popped into the oven for a few minutes, from which it emerges browned and crispy. (Even finicky Barry, not usually a fan of turkey breast, likes this dish.)

We are essentially making a Thanksgiving-quality turkey dinner in reasonable quantity (a 6-pound breast) and in less than 1 hour instead of the usual 2 to 3 hours—clearly a boon for smaller families and anyone who has ever anticipated the ritual of the holiday turkey dinner with fear and loathing.

MAKES 10 SERVINGS

1 tablespoon olive oil

1 tablespoon fresh oregano leaves

1 tablespoon fresh basil leaves

1 tablespoon fresh parsley leaves

3 cloves garlic, peeled

1 teaspoon salt

1/2 teaspoon ground black pepper

1 (5 1/2- to 6-pound) fresh turkey breast

4 cups water

1 tablespoon unsalted butter

2 tablespoon instant flour

1/2 teaspoon paprika

1/4 teaspoon poultry seasoning

Combine the olive oil, oregano, basil, parsley, garlic, salt, and pepper in a food processor. Process to form a paste and work the paste under the skin of the turkey breast. Place a trivet or a small wire rack into the pressure cooker and put the turkey on it. Add the water. Cover, lock,

ELECTRIC COMPATIBLE

Too large for a 4- or 5-quart pressure cooker.

SLICING THE TURKEY

Place the turkey, skin side down, on a cutting board. On each side, slice down along the breastbone, prying the meat from the rib cage to produce two large boneless fillets. Thinly slice each crosswise.

and bring to low pressure over high heat. Reduce the heat to stabilize pressure and cook for 30 minutes.

Preheat the oven to 425F (220C).

Remove the pressure cooker from the heat and let the pressure drop naturally. Carefully remove the cover. Transfer the turkey to a roasting pan, reserving the cooking liquid in the cooker, and rub the breast all over with the butter. Brown in the oven, 15 to 20 minutes.

For the gravy, bring 4 cups of the reserved cooking liquid to a boil in a saucepan over high heat. Boil until reduced by half, about 10 minutes. Combine the flour and ¼ cup of drippings from the roasting pan in a small bowl. Add to the gravy and bring back to a boil. Stir in the paprika and poultry seasoning and boil until smooth and thick, about 1 minute. Thinly slice the turkey and serve the gravy on the side.

Chicken with Chive Dumplings

Sunday supper food at its best, chicken and dumplings takes especially well to moist pressure cooking, which yields some of the most mouthwatering, tender, and beautifully feathery dumplings we've ever had. We've timed things so that the chicken comes out of the pressure cooker just slightly undercooked; wrapped in foil, it will finish cooking on its own while you make the dumplings.

MAKES 6 SERVINGS

CHICKEN

1 (3-pound) frying chicken, cut up

10 ounces leek, trimmed to white and light green parts, sliced (about 1½ cups), and rinsed well

4 small carrots, peeled and sliced (about 1 cup)

2 stalks celery with leafy tops, sliced (about ¾ cup)

¾ cup defatted Chicken Stock (page 36 or canned)

3 large sprigs fresh thyme

1 teaspoon salt

ELECTRIC
COMPATIBLE
with Revision:

Dumplings will puff up too large for a 4- or 5-quart pressure cooker.

Cook at high pressure for 10 minutes if your cooker works only at high pressure. To make the dumplings, use the browning setting to bring the cooking liquid to a gentle boil.

½ teaspoon ground black pepper

DUMPLINGS

2 large eggs

⅔ cup skim milk

1 tablespoon baking powder

1 teaspoon salt

1 tablespoon snipped chives

2 cups all-purpose flour

For the chicken, combine the chicken, leek, carrots, celery, stock, thyme, salt, and pepper in a pressure cooker. Cover, lock, and bring to low pressure over high heat. Reduce the heat to stabilize pressure and cook for 13 minutes. (If your machine will only work at high pressure, cook for 10 minutes.)

Lower the pressure by a quick-release method. Carefully remove the cover. Remove the chicken to a plate and cover with foil to keep warm.

For the dumplings, combine the eggs, milk, baking powder, and salt in a large bowl. Whisk until frothy. Add the chives. Whisk in 1 cup of the flour, then stir in the additional cup to make a stiff batter.

Bring the liquid in the pressure cooker to a boil. Using ⅓ cup of the batter for each, drop 6 dumplings into the boiling liquid. Cover, lock, and bring to high pressure over high heat. Reduce the heat to stabilize pressure and cook for 5 minutes.

Lower the pressure by a quick-release method. Carefully remove the cover. Serve the chicken with the dumplings and cooking liquid.

ELECTRIC
COMPATIBLE
with Revision:

*Cook at high pressure for
12 minutes if your cooker
works only at high
pressure.*

Pot-au-Feu

**Think of pot-au-feu as French comfort food, sort of a cross between
Jewish chicken soup and an Asian hot pot. Pierre Franey has written
lovingly about the pot-au-feus his mother made, generally as a special
Saturday-night treat. The contents vary according to the whim and
creativity of the cook—so use this recipe as guide rather than as a
Bible. The meat can be beef or chicken, but we just think there's
something more comforting about chicken. Pair it with any full-
flavored smoked sausage, such as turkey kielbasa for a leaner dish.
Start with homemade stock for the best results; the better the stock,
the better the dish. Garnish, if desired, with some cornichons.**

MAKES 6 TO 8 SERVINGS

3 kohlrabi bulbs, peeled and each cut into 8 wedges

2 small leeks, trimmed to white and light green parts, cut into
rings, and rinsed well (about 1 cup)

8 ounces baby-cut carrots

1 (5-pound) frying chicken, cut up

14 ounces lean kielbasa, cut into chunks

4 cups defatted Chicken Stock (page 36 or canned)

¾ teaspoon dried thyme

1 teaspoon salt

½ teaspoon ground black pepper

Put the kohlrabi on the bottom of a pressure cooker. Add the remaining ingredients. Cover, lock, and bring to low pressure over high heat.
Reduce the heat to stabilize pressure and cook for 15 minutes. (If your
machine will only work at high pressure, cook for 10 to 12 minutes.)

Lower the pressure by a quick-release method. Carefully remove
the cover. Serve the chicken, sausage, and vegetables on a large, deep
platter. Skim fat from the stock and serve the stock on the side in a
gravy boat.

Chicken Curry

We love the versatility of curry; vary the strength of powder used and you have essentially a different dish. Curry powder is actually an English invention, a spice blend that seasons food in the manner of complex Indian masala mixtures. Because the coconut milk sauce in this recipe can burn easily, we recommend using a flame tamer, a handy gadget available in most hardware stores, to temper the heat beneath a manual pressure cooker. For the same reason, we do not recommend making this dish in a cooker that will work only on high pressure.

ELECTRIC
COMPATIBLE
with Revision:

Compatible only if your cooker works at low pressure.

MAKES 4 SERVINGS

1 medium red bell pepper, cut into $\frac{1}{2}$-inch squares (about 1 cup)

1 medium green bell pepper, cut into $\frac{1}{2}$-inch squares (about 1 cup)

1 large red potato, cut into $\frac{1}{2}$-inch cubes (about $1\frac{2}{3}$ cups)

2 small yellow onions, cut into $\frac{1}{2}$-cubes (about $1\frac{1}{3}$ cups)

1 (14-ounce) can light coconut milk

3 tablespoons Curry Powder (page 32 or purchased)

1 tablespoon grated fresh ginger

$\frac{1}{2}$ cup water

$\frac{1}{2}$ cup golden raisins

6 (5-ounce) chicken thighs, skin and visible fat removed

Combine all ingredients in a pressure cooker. Cover, lock, and bring to low pressure over medium heat. Adjust the heat to stabilize pressure and cook for 10 minutes.

Lower the pressure by a quick-release method. Carefully remove the cover.

ELECTRIC
COMPATIBLE
with Revision:

*Cook at high pressure for
12 minutes if your cooker
works only at high
pressure.*

HOW TO CUT UP A CHICKEN

Place the chicken on a
cutting board, breast
side down, and make
two slits the entire
length of the bird, one
on each side of the
backbone. Remove
and reserve the back-
bone, along with the
neck and giblets that
will have come pack-
aged with the chicken
(for soup making).
Butterfly the bird
open, turn bone side
down, and press down
lightly to flatten.
Using poultry shears
or a sturdy knife, cut
the chicken in half
lengthwise through
the breastbone. Cut
off and reserve the

Chicken Cacciatore

**Our all-time favorite food extravaganza is the annual Ninth Avenue
festival in Manhattan. One weekend each summer, almost a mile of
this gritty thoroughfare—just above what remains of an old food dis-
trict that once boasted storefront after storefront with whole roast
ducks and suckling pigs hanging in windows, bins of aromatic spices
crowding sales floors, and some of the city's best-kept restaurant
finds hidden in back of modest shops—is closed to traffic to accommodate dozens of restaurant food kiosks. When Kevin lived around
the corner from Ninth Avenue, he would virtually fast for days to be
able to eat his way up one side of Ninth and down the other all
weekend.**

**Although the fair offers the requisite selection of Italian sausage
sandwiches and calzones, it also boasts the offerings of some wonderful neighborhood restaurants, one of our favorites of which for years
served up the best cacciatore, or hunter's stew, around. Our version is
made with capers instead of olives—use the larger, more flavorful Italian capers rather than the petite French nonpareils—and has a touch
of rosemary. We like to make it a day in advance and let the flavors
meld overnight in the refrigerator.**

MAKES 6 SERVINGS

1/2 tablespoon olive oil

1 (3- to 3 1/2-pound) frying chicken, cut up

1 medium yellow onion, cut into thin wedges

1 medium red bell pepper, cut into thin strips

1 medium green bell pepper, cut into thin strips

8 ounces white button mushrooms, cleaned, stemmed, and cut
into wedges

4 cloves garlic, minced

1/2 cup dry white wine

1 (14 1/2-ounce) can diced tomatoes

1 tablespoon large capers, drained

2 tablespoons chopped fresh rosemary or 2 teaspoons dried
rosemary

1 tablespoon chopped fresh oregano or 1 teaspoon dried oregano

½ teaspoon salt

½ teaspoon ground black pepper

Preheat a pressure cooker over medium heat and swirl in the oil. In batches, brown all pieces of chicken on both sides, about 10 minutes.

Remove the chicken to a plate and add the onion, bell peppers, mushrooms, and garlic to the cooker. Cook, stirring constantly, until the mushrooms have softened, about 3 minutes. Add the wine and cook for 1 minute more, stirring to dislodge any browned bits on the bottom of the cooker. Add the tomatoes, capers, rosemary, oregano, salt, and black pepper. Cover, lock, and bring to low pressure over high heat. Reduce the heat to stabilize pressure and cook for 15 minutes. (If your machine will only work at high pressure, cook for 12 minutes.)

Lower the pressure by a quick-release method. Carefully remove the cover.

wing tips. Cut the legs from the breasts and then cut each leg at the joint between the thigh and drumstick. Remove excess skin and fat from the bird.

Lemon Garlic Chicken

A much-reported book published a few years ago advocated roasting chicken at 500F (260C), which produces wonderfully crisp skin, but can leave the chicken somewhat less than fully cooked at the bone and the oven billowing smoke as fat dripping off the bird catches on fire. (More than a few neighbors, we've heard, received dinner in the way of a peace offering for smoke-filled hallways.) But by precooking chicken for 10 minutes in a pressure cooker and then finishing it in a high oven, you can enjoy crispy chicken fully cooked at the bone. The breast meat is succulent all the way through from moist pressure cooking—in a smokeless home, because the fat has already been rendered by the time the bird hits the hot oven. In addition, our method takes half the time of high oven baking alone and a third that of conventional cooking methods.

MAKES 6 SERVINGS

 ELECTRIC
COMPATIBLE:

Too large for a 4- or 5-quart cooker.

1 lemon, quartered

5 sprigs fresh parsley

5 cloves garlic, peeled

1 (3½-pound) whole frying chicken

2 cups water

1 tablespoon unsalted butter at room temperature

½ tablespoon arrowroot

1 tablespoon fresh lemon juice

2 tablespoons chopped fresh parsley

1 tablespoon grated lemon zest

Preheat the oven to 475F (245C).

Put the lemon quarters, parsley sprigs, and 4 cloves of the garlic into the cavity of the chicken. Put the chicken into a pressure cooker. Add the water. Cover, lock, and bring to high pressure over high heat. Reduce the heat to stabilize pressure and cook for 10 minutes.

Lower the pressure by a quick-release method. Carefully remove the cover. Transfer the chicken to a roasting pan, reserving the cooking liquid. Remove and discard the lemon and parsley. Remove and reserve the garlic from the cavity. Press the remaining uncooked garlic clove into the butter and rub it all over the chicken.

Roast the chicken in the oven 12 to 15 minutes, until the skin has browned, the juices run clear, and the chicken has reached an internal temperature of 170F (75C) on an instant-read thermometer. Transfer the chicken to a plate and cover with foil to keep warm.

Meanwhile, make the gravy. Strain 2 cups of the reserved cooking liquid into a medium saucepan over high heat. Press in the reserved cooked garlic. Bring to a boil and boil for 5 minutes. Dissolve the arrowroot in the lemon juice and stir the mixture into the gravy. Boil for 2 minutes, then stir in the chopped parsley and lemon zest.

Chicken and Rice

Barry was introduced to this Caribbean rendition of arroz con pollo—the classic chicken and rice dish served throughout the Spanish-speaking world—in a Cuban restaurant in Hialeah. A few years later, we often ordered a somewhat quirkier version in a Cuban/Chinese restaurant (for some reason, a not uncommon menu pairing in New York City) on the Upper West Side. It was accompanied by a Cuban "wonton" soup sprinkled with cilantro and pieces of barbecued pork into which a whole raw egg was cracked. Our recipe is closer to the original, with no wontons in sight.

ELECTRIC
COMPATIBLE
with Revision:

Cook for 9 minutes at high pressure if your cooker works only at high pressure.

MAKES 4 SERVINGS

4 (9- to 10-ounce) bone-in chicken breasts with skin

Salt to taste

Ground black pepper to taste

2 teaspoons olive oil

1 medium green bell pepper, chopped (about 1 cup)

1 medium yellow onion, chopped (about 1 cup)

1 teaspoon seeded and minced jalapeño chile

1 (14½-ounce) can diced tomatoes

1¼ cups defatted Chicken Stock (page 36 or canned)

1 cup long-grain white rice

1 teaspoon ground cumin

1 teaspoon dried oregano

3 cloves garlic, minced or peeled

½ teaspoon paprika

Season the chicken breasts with salt and black pepper.

Preheat a pressure cooker over medium-high heat and swirl in the oil. Add the chicken breasts to the cooker, skin side down, (in batches, if necessary) and cook until well browned, 5 to 7 minutes. Remove the chicken to a plate.

Add the bell pepper and onion to the cooker. Cook, stirring constantly, over medium-high heat until the onion is golden, the pepper has softened, and any browned bits have been dislodged from the bottom of the pan. Stir in the jalapeño, tomatoes, stock, rice, cumin, and oregano. Place the chicken breasts on top. Scatter minced garlic on top or press in whole cloves. Sprinkle paprika over the chicken. Cover, lock, and bring to low pressure over high heat. Reduce the heat to stabilize pressure and cook for 12 minutes. (If your machine will only work at high pressure, cook for 9 minutes.)

Lower the pressure by a quick-release method. Carefully remove the cover.

ELECTRIC
COMPATIBLE
with Revision:

Cook at high pressure for 9 minutes if your cooker works only at high pressure.

Chicken with Figs

For our rendition of chicken Véronique, we've replaced the white grapes, which unfortunately would fall apart in the pressure cooker, with figs. We're partial to the taste of Calimyrna figs, whose lighter shade more closely resembles the grapes of the original recipe, but you could also use the Mission variety. Nonfat half-and-half could easily replace the full-fat variety in this recipe.

MAKES 4 SERVINGS

2 teaspoons olive oil

4 (9- to 10-ounce) bone-in chicken breasts with skin

1 medium yellow onion, diced (about 1 cup)

3 cloves garlic, minced or peeled

8 ounces white button mushrooms, cleaned, stemmed, and sliced

3/4 teaspoon dried tarragon or 1/2 tablespoon chopped fresh tarragon

2/3 cup defatted Chicken Stock (page 36 or canned)

1/2 tablespoon paprika

12 dried Calimyrna figs, quartered, or Mission figs, halved

1/3 cup half-and-half

1 tablespoon cornstarch

Salt to taste

Ground black pepper to taste

Preheat a pressure cooker over medium-high heat and swirl in the oil. Place the chicken breasts in the cooker, skin side down, and brown (in batches, if necessary). Remove the chicken to a plate and add the onion to the cooker. Cook, stirring constantly, until translucent, about 30 seconds. Stir in minced garlic or press in whole cloves. Add the mushrooms and cook until they begin to soften, about 1½ minutes; add the tarragon. Add the stock and stir to dislodge any browned bits from the bottom of the cooker. Add the paprika and figs.

Return the chicken to the cooker and spoon some sauce over it. Cover, lock, and bring to low pressure over high heat. Reduce the heat to stabilize pressure and cook for 12 minutes. (If your machine will only work at high pressure, cook for 9 minutes.)

Meanwhile, mix the half-and-half and the cornstarch together in a small bowl.

Lower the pressure by a quick-release method. Carefully remove the cover. Stir in the cornstarch mixture and cook for 1 to 2 minutes more, until thick and bubbly. Add salt and pepper to taste.

Chicken Paprikash

We've added a bit of hot paprika to our paprikash, which perks the usually tame dish up significantly. Our version is also quite a bit healthier than the original, because we dispense with the typical first step of browning the chicken in bacon drippings and substitute reduced-fat for full-fat sour cream. Serve with broad egg noodles.

MAKES 4 SERVINGS

ELECTRIC
COMPATIBLE
with Revision:

Cook on high pressure for 9 minutes if your cooker works only at high pressure. Use the browning setting to warm the sauce.

4 (10-ounce) bone-in chicken breasts with skin

1 large yellow onion, chopped (about 1½ cups)

½ cup defatted Chicken Stock (page 36 or canned)

1 tablespoon sun-dried tomato paste

2 large cloves garlic, minced

1 tablespoon paprika

½ tablespoon hot paprika

1 teaspoon salt

2 sprigs fresh thyme

2 tablespoons all-purpose flour

1 cup reduced-fat sour cream

Put the chicken and onion into a pressure cooker. Mix together the stock, sun-dried tomato paste, garlic, paprikas, and salt in a bowl. Pour the stock mixture over the chicken and onion. Add the thyme. Cover, lock, and bring to low pressure over high heat. Reduce the heat to stabilize pressure and cook for 12 minutes. (If your machine will only work at high pressure, cook for 9 minutes.)

Lower the pressure by a quick-release method. Carefully remove the cover. Remove the chicken to a plate and cover with foil to keep warm. Transfer ¼ cup of the cooking liquid from the cooker to a small bowl and whisk in the flour. Return the mixture to the cooker and cook the sauce over medium heat, whisking constantly, until thickened, about 2 minutes. Remove from the heat and stir in the sour cream. Spoon sauce over chicken.

Seafood

Stews are our favorite seafood preparations in the pressure cooker, and we serve them up in all sorts of configurations. Fish Stew is as simple and straightforward a preparation as you'll find anywhere, a perfect example of pressure cooking at its best in preparing fresh and flavorful food in minutes. Our American Seafood Stew adds shrimp and squid to the equation, and Bouillabaisse Provençal boasts an impressive medley of fish and shellfish. Any can be prepared in less than 15 minutes.

Seafood cooks so quickly by most means that many cooks ignore the pressure cooker as an option for preparing it. We think this is a shame, because pressure cooking can improve the taste and texture of some seafood, such as salmon steaks, which are often a bit dry when cooked by conventional means. Pressure cooking also allows you to speed up the preparation of other, traditionally longer-cooking ingredients in the dish and add the fish or shellfish at the last minute.

Our sampling of pressure-cooked seafood recipes includes a rouxless Crab and Shrimp Gumbo (5 minutes); Halibut in Red Chard, which is made using fillets (5 minutes); Curried Mussels (7 minutes); and Jamaican Squid, our longest-cooking seafood dish at 15 minutes.

ELECTRIC
COMPATIBLE

with Revision:

*Use the browning setting to
cook the bacon and then
the vegetables.*

American Seafood Stew

**This spicy concoction is a cross between a Caribbean stew, boasting a
healthy dose of jalapeño chile and cayenne pepper, and a tomato-
based San Francisco cioppino. Sometimes we serve it with rice, which
tempers the heat a bit. On one of our frequent forays into the Chesapeake Bay region, we developed this recipe with a local delicacy called
rockfish. It's actually a member of the bass family, not the ocean
perch from the Pacific that is more commonly referred to as rockfish;
you could substitute either striped or sea bass. Barry always serves a
bottle of pepper sauce on the side, a habit he acquired when he lived
in St. Thomas.**

MAKES 6 SERVINGS

1 teaspoon olive oil

4 slices bacon, chopped

1 large yellow onion, chopped (about 1¼ cups)

1 medium green bell pepper, chopped (about 1 cup)

6 cloves garlic, finely minced

2 small tomatoes, peeled, seeded, and chopped (about 1 cup) or
1 (14½-ounce) can diced tomatoes, drained

½ teaspoon cayenne pepper

1 teaspoon chopped jalapeño chile

2 teaspoons dried thyme or 2 tablespoons fresh thyme

2 cups Fish Stock (page 40 or frozen) or clam juice

¾ cup dry white wine

3 bay leaves

1 (4 × 1-inch) strip orange zest

8 ounces medium shrimp, peeled and deveined

1 (1½-pound) rockfish or bass fillet, cut into 6 chunks

1½ pounds littleneck clams (about 18), scrubbed

8 ounces bay scallops

8 ounces cleaned squid bodies, cut into 1-inch rings

Preheat a pressure cooker over medium heat and swirl in the oil. Add the bacon and cook, stirring constantly, until just beginning to color, about 2 minutes. Add the onion, bell pepper, and garlic. Still stirring constantly, cook until the bell pepper is very limp, about 5 minutes. Add the tomatoes, cayenne, jalapeño, thyme, stock or juice, wine, bay leaves, and orange zest. Cover, lock, and bring to high pressure over high heat. Reduce the heat to stabilize pressure and cook for 10 minutes.

Lower the pressure by a quick-release method. Carefully remove the cover. Stir in the shrimp, rockfish, and clams. Re-cover, lock, and bring back to high pressure over high heat. Reduce the heat to stabilize pressure, and cook for 3 minutes.

Lower the pressure by a quick-release method. Carefully remove the cover. Stir in the scallops and squid. Cover (but do not lock) the cooker and cook over low heat until the squid and scallops are opaque, about 1 minute.

Bouillabaisse Provençal

A simple Provençal fishermen's stew that makes a meal fit for a king, this recipe should be considered as a point of departure. Use the freshest fish available, adding or substituting any firm-fleshed fish or well-scrubbed clams for the fish and shellfish we call for. It boasts a slight licorice undertone from the fennel seeds and anise liqueur; traditionally French Pernod or Ricard, but Greek ouzo would work just as well. Place the fennel seeds between sheets of wax paper and crush them lightly with a rubber mallet or rolling pin to release their flavor. The dish is usually made using a fair amount of saffron. We augment comparatively expensive saffron with turmeric (sometimes called the "poor man's saffron"); in a pinch, skip the saffron entirely and boost the ration of turmeric a bit. Serve the stew over slices of toasted French bread or Garlic Cheese Croutons (page 28).

MAKES 6 SERVINGS

ELECTRIC COMPATIBLE

with Revision:

Use the browning setting to cook the vegetables.

1 tablespoon olive oil

1 medium yellow onion, diced (about 1 cup)

4 ounces leek, trimmed to white and light green parts, sliced, and rinsed well (about ½ cup packed)

1 medium carrot, peeled and diced (about ⅓ cup)

2 large stalks celery, diced (about ⅔ cup)

8 large cloves garlic, minced

⅓ cup dry vermouth

1 teaspoon fennel seeds, lightly crushed

1 teaspoon ground turmeric

¼ teaspoon saffron threads, crumbled

1 large or 2 small tomatoes, peeled, seeded, and diced (about ¾ cup)

4 cups Fish Stock (page 40 or frozen) or clam juice

2 (8-ounce) swordfish steaks, each cut into thirds

4 (6-ounce) pieces monkfish, each cut into thirds

1 pound large shrimp, shells slit open along the large curve and deveined

1 pound mussels, scrubbed

8 ounces sea scallops

2 tablespoons Pernod, Ricard, or ouzo liqueur

2 tablespoons snipped fresh dill

Heat the oil in a pressure cooker over medium heat. Add the onion, leek, carrot, celery, and garlic. Cook, stirring constantly, until the carrot softens, about 3 minutes. Stir in the vermouth, fennel seeds, turmeric, saffron, tomatoes, and fish stock or clam juice. Cover, lock, and bring to high pressure over high heat. Reduce the heat to stabilize pressure and cook for 7 minutes.

Lower the pressure by a quick-release method. Carefully remove the cover. Add the swordfish, monkfish, shrimp, mussels, and scallops. Re-cover, lock, and bring back to high pressure over high heat. Reduce the heat to stabilize pressure. Cook for 2 minutes.

Lower the pressure by a quick-release method. Carefully remove the cover. Divide the fish among 6 large, shallow bowls. Stir the liqueur into the cooking liquid. Spoon over each serving and garnish with the dill.

Down-and Dirty Rouille

We like to garnish each serving of our bouillabaisse with a dollop of *rouille*, a traditional Provençal touch. Often the thick sauce is painstakingly made with a mortar and pestle, but we've adapted our version for a quick food processor preparation. Use either roasted bell peppers from a jar or ones you've roasted and peeled yourself.

MAKES ABOUT 1 CUP

$^1/_3$ cup roasted red bell peppers

4 cloves garlic, peeled

$^1/_8$ teaspoon cayenne pepper

$^1/_2$ teaspoon dried thyme or $^1/_2$ tablespoon fresh thyme

$^1/_2$ cup mayonnaise

$^1/_4$ cup unseasoned breadcrumbs

Puree the roasted peppers, garlic, cayenne, and thyme in a food processor. Add the mayonnaise and process to combine. Add the breadcrumbs and process again until well blended.

Fish Stew

One of our all-time favorites, this is a feast fit for entertaining that can be prepared in a total of 15 minutes. The recipe epitomizes what pressure cookery is all about—fast, easy, and letting simple, fresh flavors shine. The quality of the stew, however, depends on the quality of the wine you use. We suggest a good Pinot Grigio or a better Chardonnay.

ELECTRIC
COMPATIBLE
with Revision:

Use the browning setting to make the sauce and finish the stew.

1½ pounds firm white fish (such as red snapper, cod, or halibut)

8 ounces (about 12) boiling onions, peeled

12 ounces (12 to 14) petite new red potatoes, scrubbed and halved

8 ounces white button mushrooms, cleaned, stemmed, and halved

½ cup Fish Stock (page 40 or frozen) or clam juice

½ cup dry white wine

2 tablespoons instant flour

⅓ cup heavy cream

2 tablespoons chopped fresh parsley

½ teaspoon grated lemon zest

¼ teaspoon fresh thyme

1 clove garlic, minced or peeled

Ground black pepper, to taste

Combine the fish, onions, potatoes, mushrooms, stock, and wine in a pressure cooker. Cover, lock, and bring to high pressure over high heat. Reduce the heat to stabilize pressure and cook for 3 minutes.

Lower the pressure by a quick-release method. Carefully remove the cover. Transfer the fish and vegetables to a plate and set aside. Pour the cooking liquid through a strainer into a bowl and add it back to the pressure cooker.

Meanwhile, whisk together the flour and cream in a small bowl. In a second bowl, combine the parsley, lemon zest, and thyme; add minced garlic or press in a whole clove. Over medium-low heat, whisk the flour mixture into the stock in the pressure cooker. Cook for 2 to 3 minutes. Add the parsley mixture. Return the fish and vegetables to the pot and cook for about 1 minute more to warm through. Add pepper to taste.

Salmon Wraps

Some cooks don't bother with the pressure cooker for fish fillets, because they cook so fast by conventional means, but we rather like the results it produces—in this case, wonderfully moist salmon fillets. The black bean sauce, available in your supermarket's Asian section, lends an assertive, salty flavor (don't use any additional salt in the recipe) that tempers the sweetness of the fish nicely. Be sure to remove the toothpicks before serving.

MAKES 4 SERVINGS

1 tablespoon grated fresh ginger

1/2 teaspoon sesame oil

1/4 cup chopped fresh cilantro

2 large cloves garlic, peeled

4 (4-ounce) salmon fillets

4 savoy cabbage leaves

1/2 cup dry white wine

2 tablespoons black bean sauce with garlic

1 teaspoon rice vinegar

1 green onion, trimmed to white and light green parts and chopped (about 2 tablespoons)

In a small bowl, combine the ginger, sesame oil, and cilantro. Press in the garlic. Place a salmon fillet on an end of each of the cabbage leaves and top each with about 1½ tablespoons of the ginger paste. Fold the leaves over to enclose and secure with toothpicks.

Combine the wine, black bean sauce, vinegar, and green onion in a pressure cooker. Bring to a boil over high heat. Add the stuffed cabbage leaves. Cover, lock, and bring to high pressure over high heat. Reduce the heat to stabilize pressure and cook for 5 minutes.

Lower the pressure by a quick-release method. Carefully remove the cover. Top each serving with a scant 1/4 cup of the sauce from the cooker.

ELECTRIC
COMPATIBLE
with Revision:

Use the browning setting to bring the wine and black bean sauce to a gentle boil.

ELECTRIC
COMPATIBLE

Crab and Shrimp Gumbo

We like to think of this thick, stewlike dish as an instant-gratification gumbo, whipped up in the pressure cooker in just 5 minutes. No messing around with a complicated roux; this gumbo uses filé powder as a thickener. (For an even thicker, if somewhat more viscous, gumbo, add the optional okra.) It features the succulent blue crabs that proliferate in the Chesapeake region of the Atlantic and in the Gulf. Blue crabs are small and hard shelled—except for the brief season when they shed their shells. You can buy them live in many Asian markets or frozen in supermarkets (cooked and uncooked crab would work equally well in this recipe). If you live in the Pacific Northwest, substitute a Dungeness crab, cleaned and cut up, if you prefer.

MAKES 4 SERVINGS

3 (8-ounce) blue crabs, cleaned and quartered

8 ounces medium shrimp, peeled and deveined

1 large yellow onion, diced (about 1½ cups)

1 large green bell pepper, diced (about 1½ cups)

1 whole red finger chile

1 cup Fish Stock (page 40 or frozen) or clam juice

1 bay leaf

½ teaspoon dried thyme

¼ teaspoon ground cumin

8 ounces okra, trimmed and cut into ½-inch rings (about 1¾ cups) (optional)

8 to 12 drops green hot sauce, to taste

1 tablespoon gumbo filé powder

2 cloves garlic, minced or peeled

2 cups cooked long-grain white rice

Lime wedges, for garnish

Combine the crabs, shrimp, onion, bell pepper, chile, stock or clam juice, bay leaf, thyme, cumin, and okra, if desired, in a pressure cooker.

Cover, lock, and bring to high pressure over high heat. Reduce the heat to stabilize pressure and cook for 5 minutes.

Lower the pressure by a quick-release method. Carefully remove the cover. Discard the chile and stir in the hot sauce and filé powder. Stir in the minced garlic or press in whole cloves. Put ½ cup rice in each of 4 bowls and ladle the gumbo over the rice. Serve with lime wedges on the side.

Halibut in Red Chard

Your guests will love opening up the chard wrappers to find buttery halibut fillets surrounded by carrot matchsticks. Halibut, a firm-fleshed fish from the Pacific Northwest, is one of our favorites. Choose fillets rather than steaks so there won't be any bones.

ELECTRIC
COMPATIBLE
with Revision:

Use the browning setting to bring the wine and mustard mixture to a gentle boil.

MAKES 4 SERVINGS

4 (6-ounce) halibut fillets

4 large red chard leaves

2 medium carrots, peeled and cut into 1-inch matchsticks (about ⅔ cup)

2 green onions, trimmed to white and light green parts and chopped (about ¼ cup)

½ cup dry white wine

1 tablespoon Dijon mustard

½ teaspoon salt

¼ teaspoon ground black pepper

Place a halibut fillet on an end of each of the chard leaves. Divide the carrots over the fillets and scatter about 1 tablespoon of green onion over each. Fold the leaves over to enclose and secure with toothpicks.

Mix together the wine, mustard, salt, and pepper in a small bowl. Pour into a pressure cooker and bring to a boil over high heat. Add the fish packets. Cover, lock, and bring to high pressure over high heat. Reduce the heat to stabilize pressure and cook for 5 minutes.

Lower the pressure by a quick-release method. Carefully remove the cover.

Jamaican Squid

ELECTRIC COMPATIBLE
with Revision:

Compatible only if your cooker works at low pressure.

This thick, stew-like one-pot meal juxtaposes the heat from the chile peppers with an underlying hint of cinnamon. If you can't find fresh okra, omit it rather than substituting frozen, which would fall apart in the pressure cooker. Look for cleaned fresh squid in a fish market or at the seafood counter of a better supermarket to avoid the nuisance of cleaning frozen squid.

The thick sauce for this dish can scorch easily; if you're using a manual pressure cooker on a gas stovetop, you may want to use a flame tamer, a device available at most hardware stores that will moderate the heat.

MAKES 4 SERVINGS

1$\frac{1}{2}$ pounds cleaned squid bodies and tentacles

12 ounces medium shrimp, peeled and deveined

8 ounces fresh whole okra, trimmed

1 cup long-grain white rice

1 medium yellow onion, chopped (about 1 cup)

1 medium stalk celery, chopped (about $\frac{1}{3}$ cup)

1 banana chile, cored, seeded, deveined, and chopped (about $\frac{1}{4}$ cup)

1 mild green chile, cored, seeded, deveined, and chopped (about $\frac{1}{4}$ cup)

1 clove garlic, minced

1 (14$\frac{1}{2}$-ounce) can diced tomatoes

1 cup Fish Stock (page 40 or frozen) or clam juice

2 tablespoons Jerk Seasoning (see opposite or purchased)

1 lime

Cut the squid bodies into ¾-inch rings. You should have about 3 cups rings and tentacles.

Combine the squid and the remaining ingredients, except for the lime, in a pressure cooker. Mix well. Cover, lock, and bring to low pressure over medium heat. Adjust the heat to stabilize pressure and cook for 15 minutes.

Remove the pressure cooker from the heat and let the pressure drop naturally. Carefully remove the cover and squeeze in the juice from the lime.

Jerk Seasoning

It's simple enough to whip up a batch of your own Caribbean spice mixture if your supermarket doesn't stock it.

MAKES ABOUT 4 TABLESPOONS

1 tablespoon plus 1 teaspoon ground allspice

1 tablespoon plus 1 teaspoon granulated light brown sugar

½ tablespoon ground ginger

½ tablespoon ground cinnamon

½ tablespoon salt

½ tablespoon ground black pepper

½ teaspoon cayenne pepper

Mix all the ingredients together well. Store in an airtight container for up to 6 months.

Salmon Steaks

Finished with a tapenade, a robust Mediterranean olive garnish, these salmon steaks are healthy, elegant enough for entertaining, and ready in less than 5 minutes! In the pressure cooker the steaks stay quite moist, with less danger of becoming overly dry than with other methods of preparation. The 8-ounce salmon steaks should be about 1 inch

 ELECTRIC COMPATIBLE

thick. **As a guide for cooking other types of fish steaks, bear in mind that the fillets should be cooked in the pressure cooker on high pressure for about 4 minutes per inch of thickness.**

MAKES 4 SERVINGS

1¼ pounds fennel, trimmed to the bulb and thinly sliced lengthwise

1 large red bell pepper, thinly sliced (about 1½ cups)

½ cup dry white wine

4 (8-ounce) salmon steaks

1 teaspoon lemon pepper

2 tablespoons pitted kalamata olives

1 tablespoon large capers, drained

1 tablespoon fresh lemon juice

½ tablespoon olive oil

1 teaspoon anchovy paste

1 teaspoon fresh flat-leaf parsley leaves

½ teaspoon grated lemon zest

Place the fennel into the bottom of a pressure cooker. Layer the bell pepper over the fennel and add the wine. Sprinkle the salmon steaks with the lemon pepper and lay them on top. Cover, lock, and bring to high pressure over high heat. Reduce the heat to stabilize pressure and cook for 4 minutes.

Meanwhile, combine the olives, capers, lemon juice, olive oil, anchovy paste, parsley, and lemon zest in a food processor or blender. Process to a coarse chop.

Lower the pressure by a quick-release method. Carefully remove the cover. Spoon a scant tablespoon of the olive garnish over each salmon steak.

Curried Mussels

Pungent Thai red curry paste lends heat to this light yet hearty stew, brimming with squash and tomatoes and ready in less than 10 minutes in the pressure cooker. It makes a substantial meal paired with a salad and a loaf of crusty bread. Be sure to ladle generous helpings of the spicy sauce from the pot over each serving of mussels.

 ELECTRIC COMPATIBLE

Most supermarket fish counters stock mussels these days. Buy debearded mussels for easy cleaning—rinse under cold running water, discarding any broken mussels and those that don't close when tapped.

MAKES 4 SERVINGS

1 (1-pound) butternut squash, peeled, seeded, and cut into chunks (about 3 cups)

1 small yellow onion, chopped (about ¾ cup)

1 (14½-ounce) can diced tomatoes

¼ cup dry white wine

1 tablespoon Thai red curry paste

2 pounds mussels

Combine the squash, onion, tomatoes, wine, and curry paste in a pressure cooker. Cover, lock, and bring to high pressure over high heat. Reduce the heat to stabilize pressure and cook for 5 minutes.

Lower the pressure by a quick-release method. Carefully remove the cover. Add the mussels, re-cover, lock, and bring back to high pressure over high heat. Reduce the heat to stabilize pressure and cook for 2 minutes.

Lower the pressure by a quick-release method. Carefully remove the cover. Before serving, discard any mussels that have not opened.

Creole Crab and Rice Stew

ELECTRIC COMPATIBLE *with Revision:*

Use the browning setting to sauté the vegetables and toast the rice.

This spicy stew is a bit like a wet risotto with a Louisiana accent. A satisfying main course, it can also serve six as a side dish. It's particularly rich and tasty made with homemade Smoked Turkey Stock. The crabmeat can be fresh, frozen, or canned.

MAKES 4 SERVINGS

1/2 tablespoon olive oil

1 small yellow onion, finely chopped (about 1/2 cup)

1 large green bell pepper, finely chopped (about 1 1/4 cups)

2 cloves garlic, minced

1 cup Arborio rice

2 1/4 cups Smoked Turkey Stock (page 38), Turkey Stock (page 38), or defatted Chicken Stock (page 36 or canned)

1 small tomato, peeled, seeded, and chopped (about 2/3 cup)

1/2 tablespoon Creole Seasoning (page 77 or purchased)

1/2 teaspoon dried thyme

5 ounces lump crabmeat (about 1/2 cup), picked over

Hot sauce to taste

2 tablespoons chopped fresh parsley

Combine the oil, onion, bell pepper, and garlic in a pressure cooker over high heat. Sauté until the onion begins to turn golden, about 4 minutes. Add the rice and cook, stirring constantly, for about 1 minute more to lightly toast it. Stir in the stock, tomato, Creole seasoning, and thyme. Cover, lock, and bring to high pressure over high heat. Reduce the heat to stabilize pressure and cook for 6 minutes.

Lower the pressure by a quick-release method. Carefully remove the cover. Stir in the crabmeat and hot sauce. Set aside, uncovered, for about 5 minutes, until most of the liquid has been absorbed by the rice. Sprinkle each serving with parsley.

Fish in Agua Loco

Fish poached in "crazy water," a spicy tomato broth seasoned with crushed red pepper, is popular throughout the Mediterranean basin—it's called fish in *acqua pazza* in Italy and fish in *agua loco* in Spain and in the trendy hybrid Chicago restaurant where we first sampled it. It can be made from whole fish, fillets (which we use here), or a mixture of seafood.

ELECTRIC COMPATIBLE
with Revision:

Use the browning setting to bring the cooking liquid to a gentle boil.

MAKES 4 SERVINGS

2 medium tomatoes, peeled, seeded, and chopped (about $1\frac{1}{2}$ cups) or 1 ($14\frac{1}{2}$-ounce) can diced tomatoes

$\frac{1}{2}$ cup dry white wine

1 small jalapeño chile, cored, seeded, deveined, and chopped (about 1 tablespoon)

$\frac{1}{4}$ teaspoon crushed red pepper flakes

$\frac{1}{4}$ cup chopped fresh cilantro

4 (8-ounce) firm white fish fillets (such as hoki, other cod, or halibut)

Combine the tomatoes, wine, jalapeño, pepper flakes, and 2 tablespoons of the cilantro in a pressure cooker. Bring to a boil over high heat. Add the fish. Cover, lock, and bring to high pressure over high heat. Reduce the heat to stabilize pressure and cook for 3 minutes.

Lower the pressure by a quick-release method. Carefully remove the cover. Place each fillet into a warmed soup plate and pour $\frac{1}{2}$ cup of the cooking liquid over it. Sprinkle each serving with $\frac{1}{2}$ tablespoon of the remaining cilantro.

ELECTRIC
COMPATIBLE
with Revision:

*Use the browning setting to
sauté the vegetables and
bring to a gentle boil.*

Gingered Clams and Mushrooms

**Somewhat evocative of a Chinese clam casserole, which is steamed in
a clay pot, Gingered Clams and Mushrooms has a definite Asian
accent. In the traditional dish, however, the clams are added to a
longer-cooked sauce. In our pressure cooker version, the clams cook
in the sauce and are infused with its flavor. Serve with crusty bread
for dunking.**

MAKES 4 SERVINGS

½ tablespoon olive oil

4 ounces leek, trimmed to white and light green parts, sliced,
and rinsed well (about ⅔ cup)

2 cloves garlic, minced

2 tablespoons grated fresh ginger

1 small jalapeño chile, cored, seeded, deveined, and chopped
(about 1 tablespoon)

8 ounces white button mushrooms, cleaned, stemmed, and larger
mushrooms halved or quartered

⅔ cup clam juice, Fish Stock (page 40 or frozen), defatted
Chicken Stock (page 36 or canned), or water

2 tablespoons dry sherry

3 pounds littleneck clams (about 36), scrubbed

Preheat a pressure cooker over medium heat and swirl in the oil. Add
the leek and cook, stirring occasionally, until very limp and just beginning to color, about 4 minutes. Stir in the garlic and cook until fragrant, about 30 seconds. Stir in the ginger. Add the jalapeño,
mushrooms, juice, stock or water, and the sherry. Increase the heat to
high and bring to a boil. Add the clams. Cover, lock, and bring to high
pressure over high heat. Reduce the heat to stabilize pressure and cook
for 1 minute.

Lower the pressure by a quick-release method. Carefully remove
the cover. If some clams have not opened, re-cover (but do not lock)
and cook over high heat for about 1 minute. Discard any clams that
have still not opened. Divide the clams and mushrooms among 4

large shallow bowls and add about ⅓ cup of the cooking liquid to each serving.

VARIATION

Hot Pot: The flavorful broth in which we cook Gingered Clams and Mushrooms also works well as the basis for a Vietnamese hot pot for 6. Double all ingredients in the original recipe other than the mushrooms and clams. When you add the mushrooms and clam juice to the cooker, also add 1 pound chicken breast meat, diced. After the clams have been added and the dish pressure cooked, stir in 6 ounces presoaked rice stick vermicelli and 1½ cups bean sprouts. Transfer the contents of the cooker to a large serving bowl and garnish with 2 green onions, sliced on the diagonal, and 2 tablespoons chopped fresh cilantro.

Vegetables

A pressure cooker is a vegetable lover's best friend. The most scrumptious artichokes in the world emerge from the cooker in 12 minutes, complete with their wonderfully rich cooking sauce. Orange-Ginger Sweet Potato Puree, good enough to accompany the Thanksgiving turkey, takes 8 minutes; Maple-Glazed Root Vegetables, fit to shine beside the Easter ham, take 6 minutes. An aromatic Chile Verde Chili, infused with several different varieties of chiles and chock-full of pork, pressure cooks for 25 minutes instead of simmering for hours.

Even long-cooking squashes are ready in minutes. Our Spicy Curried Squash, brimming with chunks of acorn squash, cooks for 3 minutes, and Spaghetti Squash—a vegetable main course with almost no fat and about a sixth the carbohydrates of the pasta after which it is named—cooks for 15 minutes.

Pressure cooking not only saves time but also reduces the number of steps involved in preparing many vegetable recipes. Italian-style Cauliflower with Olives and Onions, which usually involves boiling and then sautéing, is a single step 5-minute recipe in the cooker. Ratatouille, the preparation of which typically involves several steps that take close to 1 hour, is done in a single step in just about 4 minutes.

Potatoes are no exception to the pattern. Comforting Horseradish Mashed Potatoes cook in 8 minutes, Dilled Potatoes, perfect by themselves or for a summertime potato salad, 3 minutes.

The pressure cooker yields robustly flavorful and nutritious vegetables and also allows the preparation of many in considerably less time than cooking by conventional methods. Here are guidelines for steaming a wide range of vegetables; we've eliminated only the few, such as pearl onions, spinach, and tomatoes that are better or quicker cooked on the stovetop.

When prepping vegetables for the pressure cooker, cut them into equal-sized pieces. If you are going to be cooking more than one vegetable at a time, try to pair vegetables with similar cooking times; cut longer-cooking vegetables into smaller pieces. Always use at least the minimum amount of water recommended by your pressure cooker's manufacturer for cooking vegetables (the amount needed will vary for different models).

Place the vegetables into a steamer basket or on a trivet or a small wire rack. Unless otherwise noted, lower the pressure by a quick-release method. Our cooking times, which are based on the time it takes for the vegetables to steam once pressure has been reached, are estimates. If a vegetable is not cooked enough for your taste, simply re-cover the cooker, lock it, and cook for 1 or 2 minutes more.

Cooking Vegetables in the Pressure Cooker

VEGETABLE	PRESSURE TO USE	MINUTES COOKED
Artichokes		
Jumbo, halved	High	10–12
Large, whole	High	10–12
Medium, whole	High	6–8
Baby, whole	High	3–5
Asparagus spears		
Thick	High	1–2
Thin	High	1
Beans, fresh		
Fava, shelled	High	1–2

VEGETABLE	PRESSURE TO USE	MINUTES COOKED
Beans (*continued*)		
Green	Low	2–3
Lima, shelled	High	1–2
Wax	Low	2–3
Beets, red or golden		
Large, whole	High	14–16
Small, whole	High	10–12
$1/2$-inch slices	High	3–4
Broccoli		
Spears	High	3–4
Florets	Low	2–3
Brussels sprouts, whole	High	3–5
Cabbage, red, white, or savoy		
Quartered	High	3–4
Shredded	High	1–2
Carrots		
2-inch cubes or baby-cut	High	3–5
$1/4$- to $1/2$-inch slices	High	1–$1^1/2$
Cauliflower		
Whole	High	5–7
Florets	High	2–4
Corn		
On the cob	High	2–3
Kernels	Low	1–2
Eggplant		
$1/2$-inch cubes	High	2–3
$1/4$-inch slices	High	1–2
Greens, shredded or chopped		
Beet	Low	2–3
Chard, red or green	High	2–3
Collard	High	4–6
Escarole	High	1–2

(*continued*)

VEGETABLE	PRESSURE TO USE	MINUTES COOKED
Greens, shredded or chopped (*continued*)		
Kale	High	1–2
Mustard	High	3–5
Kohlrabi, 1-inch cubes	High	3–5
Okra, small, whole	High	2–3
Onions, small, whole	High	2–3
Parsnips		
1-inch cubes	High	2–4
$^{1}/_{2}$-inch slices	Low	1–1$^{1}/_{2}$
Potatoes*		
New, red or white		
Medium, whole	High	6–7
Small, whole	High	4–5
Red, medium		
Whole	High	15–17
Halved	High	9–11
2-inch cubes	High	6–8
Sweet, medium		
Whole	High	15–17
Halved	High	8–10
1$^{1}/_{2}$- to 2-inch cubes	High	5–7
White, medium		
Whole	High	14–16
Halved	High	8–10
1$^{1}/_{2}$- to 2-inch cubes	High	5–7
Rutabaga, 1-inch cubes	High	4–6
Squash		
Acorn, halved	High	6–8
Butternut, $^{1}/_{2}$- to 1-inch cubes	High	3–4
Chayote, 1-inch cubes	High	1–2

*When pressure cooking potatoes, don't bring water to a boil before covering and locking the cooker; you want to bring cold water to pressure. Lowering the pressure by a quick-release method may cause potato skins to crack; if you want the skins to remain intact, remove the cooker from the heat and allow the pressure to drop naturally.

VEGETABLE	PRESSURE TO USE	MINUTES COOKED
Squash (*continued*)		
Crookneck, 1-inch cubes	High	2–3
Hubbard, $1/2$- to 1-inch cubes	High	3–5
Pattypan, whole	High	9–11
Pumpkin, 2-inch cubes	High	11–13
Spaghetti, halved	High	14–16
Zucchini, 1-inch cubes	High	2–3
Turnips		
Small, whole	High	6–8
Large, quartered	High	2–4
$1/2$-inch slices	High	1–3

Artichokes with Capers

Pressure cooking artichokes pares preparation time by up to 45 minutes. And there's no need to prepare a separate dipping sauce for artichokes cooked this way—simply pour the flavorful cooking liquid on top after plating. For this delectable appetizer or side dish, we prefer to use jumbo artichokes, which should be cut in half to ensure even cooking. If you substitute a smaller variety, cook them whole.

MAKES 4 SERVINGS

2 (1-pound) artichokes

1 lemon wedge

1 tablespoon olive oil

2 cloves garlic, chopped

2 medium green onions, trimmed to white and light green parts, and chopped (about 2 tablespoons)

2 teaspoons all-purpose flour

1 cup dry white wine

1 tablespoon fresh lemon juice

2 tablespoons chopped fresh parsley

2 tablespoons capers, drained

1/4 teaspoon crushed red pepper flakes (optional)

Remove the stems from the artichokes and cut off the pointed tips of the leaves. Slice each artichoke in half vertically and remove the fuzzy inner choke with a spoon. Rub the cut sides with the lemon wedge.

Combine the olive oil, garlic, and green onions in a pressure cooker over high heat. Cook, stirring constantly, until the garlic begins to brown, about 1 minute. Stir in the flour and cook, stirring, for about 10 seconds, just until the flour begins to darken. Add the wine and lemon juice and stir to dislodge any browned bits stuck to the bottom of the cooker. Stir in the parsley and capers. Add the artichokes. If desired, sprinkle the pepper flakes on top. Cover, lock, and bring the cooker to high pressure over high heat. Reduce the heat to stabilize pressure and cook for 12 minutes.

Lower the pressure by a quick-release method. Carefully remove the cover. Serve each artichoke in a shallow bowl, drizzled with cooking liquid.

Ginger Beets

We love cooking beets in the pressure cooker—they come out firm, but their skins slide right off. Because you will be using the cooking liquid as a sauce, be sure to scrub the beets well before cooking. This side dish, which can be served either hot or at room temperature, has a slight bite derived from the fresh ginger.

ELECTRIC
COMPATIBLE
with Revision:

Use the browning setting to bring the cooking liquid and cornstarch mixture to a gentle boil.

MAKES 6 SERVINGS

4 large beets (about 1¾ pounds total), trimmed of all greens and stalks and scrubbed

3 slices fresh ginger, each about the size of a quarter, plus ¾ teaspoon grated fresh ginger

1 cup fresh orange juice

1 tablespoon cornstarch

¼ cup granulated light brown sugar

½ teaspoon salt

¼ teaspoon ground black pepper

Combine the beets, ginger slices, and orange juice in a pressure cooker. Cover, lock, and bring to high pressure over high heat. Reduce the heat to stabilize pressure and cook for 15 minutes.

Lower the pressure by a quick-release method. Carefully remove the cover. Remove the beets to a bowl, discarding the ginger. As soon as the beets are cool enough to handle, peel, and cut into ¼-inch-thick slices.

Remove 2 tablespoons of the liquid from the cooker to a small bowl and dissolve the cornstarch in it. Return the mixture to the cooker, along with the brown sugar, grated ginger, salt, and pepper. Bring to a boil over high heat and cook, stirring, until thick and clear, 2 to 3 minutes. Stir the beets back in to coat, then serve.

VARIATION

Ginger Beet Salad: For a refreshing salad, discard the cooking liquid and chill the cooked beets for at least 2 hours. Peel and slice them. Line each of 6 chilled salad plates with 2 green lettuce leaves and fan the sliced beets over the lettuce. For a dressing, combine 2 tablespoons orange juice, 1 tablespoon canola oil, ¼ teaspoon ground ginger, a pinch of ground white pepper, and a pinch of salt in a small bowl. Blend with a whisk or a hand-held immersible blender and drizzle over the beets. Garnish with chopped green onion.

Cauliflower with Olives and Onion

ELECTRIC
COMPATIBLE
with Revision:

Use the browning setting to bring the vermouth mixture to a gentle boil before adding the cauliflower.

This simple Italian preparation would normally be prepared by first boiling cauliflower and then sautéing it with the olives and onion, a sequence significantly shortened by pressure cooking. Choose assertively flavored olives packed in brine, the type usually sold in bulk at the deli counter of better supermarkets alongside the imported cheeses, rather than the milder variety of green olives, typically stuffed and sold in jars. Look for precracked olives for easier pitting.

MAKES 6 SERVINGS

> 1 small yellow onion, sliced (about ¾ cup)
>
> 8 large green olives packed in brine, pitted and chopped
>
> ½ cup dry vermouth
>
> Cauliflower, trimmed and cut into florets about 3 inches across at the top (about 4 cups)

Combine the onion, olives, and vermouth in a pressure cooker. Bring to a boil over high heat. Add the cauliflower. Cover, lock, and bring to high pressure over high heat. Reduce the heat to stabilize pressure and cook for 5 minutes.

Lower the pressure by a quick-release method. Carefully remove the cover. Spoon into a serving bowl.

Maple-Glazed Root Vegetables

Given the rarity of root vegetable dishes, we're always pleased to find one—and even more pleased to offer this unusual rendition, in which the parsnip breaks down to both thicken and flavor the sauce, leaving chunks of the sweeter carrot and turnip-like rutabaga intact. It's the perfect accompaniment to an Easter ham. Be sure to peel off the wax coating usually put on rutabagas to preserve shelf life.

 ELECTRIC COMPATIBLE
with Revision:

Use the browning setting for the final cooking steps after releasing the pressure.

MAKES 6 SERVINGS

> 12 ounces rutabaga, peeled and cut into ¾-inch cubes (about 2 cups)
>
> 1 medium parsnip, peeled and cut into ¾-inch cubes (about 1½ cups)
>
> 3 small carrots, peeled and cut into ¾-inch cubes (about 1 cup)
>
> ¾ cup defatted Chicken Stock (page 36 or canned)
>
> ¼ cup pure maple syrup
>
> ½ teaspoon salt
>
> ¼ teaspoon ground black pepper
>
> 1 tablespoon chopped fresh parsley

Combine the rutabaga, parsnip, carrots, and stock in a pressure cooker. Cover, lock, and bring to high pressure over high heat. Reduce the heat to stabilize pressure and cook for 6 minutes.

Lower the pressure by a quick-release method. Carefully remove the cover. Bring to a boil, uncovered, over high heat and boil until most of the liquid has evaporated, about 3 minutes. Stir in the maple syrup, salt, and pepper. Cook until the parsnip has fallen apart and the maple syrup thickened, 45 to 60 seconds. Stir in the parsley and serve.

Hot Braised Eggplant

ELECTRIC
COMPATIBLE
with Revision:

Use the browning setting to thicken the sauce.

This rather spicy side dish really perks up plain roasted chicken; it's also good spooned over white rice. All of the sauces used to flavor the eggplant—the Thai roasted red chili paste, the Chinese spicy garlic sauce, and the fish sauce—can be found in the Asian section of most supermarkets these days.

MAKES 6 SERVINGS

1 (1-pound) purple eggplant or 4 baby eggplant (about 1 pound total), cut into 1-inch chunks

1 medium yellow onion, cut into 1-inch chunks

3 large cloves garlic, minced

⅓ cup dry white wine

2 tablespoons fish sauce

2 tablespoons reduced-sodium soy sauce

1 tablespoon Thai roasted red chili paste

1 tablespoon spicy garlic sauce

1 tablespoon chopped fresh ginger

½ tablespoon cornstarch dissolved in 1 tablespoon water

1 green onion, trimmed to white and light green parts, and chopped (about 2 tablespoons)

2 tablespoons chopped fresh cilantro

Combine the eggplant, onion, garlic, wine, fish sauce, soy sauce, chili paste, garlic sauce, and ginger in a pressure cooker. Cover, lock, and bring to high pressure over high heat. Reduce the heat to stabilize pressure and cook for 3 minutes.

Lower the pressure by a quick-release method. Carefully remove the cover. Stir in the cornstarch and water mixture and return the cooker to medium-low heat. Cook, stirring constantly, until thick and glossy, about 2 minutes. Stir in the green onion and cilantro and serve.

Broccoli with Tomatoes

ELECTRIC
COMPATIBLE

This side dish is cooked in the Italian tradition, a little longer than we would normally do; if you prefer your broccoli a bit more on the crunchy side, cook for only 6 minutes. It goes well with just about any broiled or grilled poultry or seafood. We are particularly fond of serving it with Chicken with Chive Dumplings (page 94).

MAKES 4 SERVINGS

12 ounces broccoli (about 2 stalks)

1 large tomato, peeled, seeded, and chopped (about 1½ cups)

1 small yellow onion, chopped (about ¾ cup)

1 large clove garlic, chopped

Pinch of crushed red pepper flakes

½ cup dry white wine

¼ teaspoon salt

Remove the broccoli florets from the stalks and cut them into bite-sized pieces. Halve the stalks lengthwise and chop them. Combine in a pressure cooker with the remaining ingredients. Cover, lock, and bring to high pressure over high heat. Reduce the heat to stabilize pressure and cook for 10 minutes.

Lower the pressure by a quick-release method. Carefully remove the cover. Spoon into a serving bowl.

ELECTRIC
COMPATIBLE

Ratatouille

The various components of ratatouille, the classic Provençal vegetable casserole, are usually partially cooked separately, then combined and cooked some more, the combination of steps totaling at least 40 to 50 minutes. Here, they cook together in 5 minutes. The dish also works well as a pasta sauce; serve with about 1 pound cooked thin-strand pasta, such as linguine or fettuccine, and add a little Parmesan cheese and crushed red pepper.

MAKES 8 TO 10 SERVINGS

1 (1-pound) purple eggplant, peeled and cut into 1-inch chunks (about 4 cups)

1 (1-pound) zucchini, peeled and cut into 1-inch chunks (about 3 cups)

2 large tomatoes, peeled, seeded, and cut into 1-inch chunks (about 1½ cups)

1 large yellow onion, peeled and cut into 1-inch chunks (about 1½ cups)

1 medium green bell pepper, cut into 1-inch chunks (about 1 cup)

½ cup water

½ cup roughly chopped fresh basil

½ tablespoon roughly chopped sun-dried tomatoes (dry pack)

3 cloves garlic, peeled

1 tablespoon fresh lemon juice

1 teaspoon salt

½ teaspoon ground black pepper

Combine the eggplant, zucchini, fresh tomatoes, onion, bell pepper, and water in a pressure cooker. Cover, lock, and bring to high pressure over high heat. Reduce the heat to stabilize pressure and cook for 4 minutes.

Lower the pressure by a quick-release method. Carefully remove the cover. Remove 1 cup of the vegetables to the bowl of a food processor and add the remaining ingredients. Process until finely chopped. Stir the mixture back into the pressure cooker. Allow to cool. Serve at room temperature or chilled.

Spaghetti Squash

Topped with a flavorful parsley, cilantro, and garlic pesto, this dish can also serve two as a filling vegetarian main course. We halve the rather large spaghetti squash before cooking so that it will fit into smaller-capacity electric or manual cookers and to facilitate safe retrieval once cooked. If you have a large enough cooker and would prefer to cook the squash whole—in which case it will not have to be drained, because the shell will keep moisture out—cook it for 20 minutes.

 ELECTRIC
COMPATIBLE

MAKES 6 SERVINGS

1 (3½-pound) spaghetti squash, halved lengthwise and seeded

1 cup water

½ cup fresh flat-leaf parsley leaves

½ cup fresh cilantro leaves

3 cloves garlic, peeled

¼ cup olive oil

½ teaspoon salt

¼ teaspoon ground black pepper

Put a trivet or a small wire rack into a pressure cooker and place the squash halves on the trivet. Add the water. Close, lock, and bring to high pressure over high heat. Reduce the heat to stabilize pressure and cook for 15 minutes.

Remove the pressure cooker from the heat and let the pressure drop naturally. Carefully remove the cover and transfer the squash to a work surface. Scrape the flesh from the shell with the tines of a fork. Place the flesh into a strainer and drain excess liquid, reserving ¼ cup. Remove the flesh to a serving bowl.

Mince the parsley, cilantro, and garlic in a food processor or blender. With the machine on, drizzle the ¼ cup reserved cooking liquid and the olive oil through the feed tube. Scrape the parsley mixture into the squash, add the salt and pepper, and toss to mix.

ELECTRIC
COMPATIBLE

Spicy Curried Squash

Vibrantly colored Thai red curry paste heightens the orange hue of acorn squash. Available in supermarket Asian aisles, it is made from red chiles combined with other spices. We usually serve this dish with lime wedges alongside roasted meats. We think it makes a lively and welcome change of pace from the typical plain acorn squash baked with only a little butter and brown sugar.

MAKES 6 SERVINGS

1 (1½-pound) acorn squash, peeled, seeded, and cut into 1-inch chunks (about 2 cups)

1 large red bell pepper, cut into 1-inch chunks (about 1 cup)

1 large white onion, cut into 1-inch chunks (about ¾ cups)

1 cup water

⅓ cup defatted Chicken Stock (page 36 or canned)

1 tablespoon cornstarch

1 teaspoon red curry paste

1 tablespoon chopped green onion

2 tablespoons chopped fresh cilantro

Combine the squash, bell pepper, and onion in a steamer basket in a pressure cooker. Add the water. Cover, lock, and bring to high pressure over high heat. Reduce the heat to stabilize pressure and cook for 3 minutes.

Meanwhile, combine the stock and cornstarch in a medium non-stick skillet. Stir to dissolve the cornstarch, then stir in the curry paste. Cook, stirring often, over medium-high heat until thick and glossy, about 3 minutes.

Remove the pressure cooker from the heat and let the pressure drop naturally. Carefully remove the cover and transfer the vegetables to the skillet and toss to coat. Stir in the green onion and cilantro.

Pumpkin Puree

Autumnal and comforting, this simple puree makes a wonderful accompaniment to Roast Turkey with Gravy (page 93) and also works well with just about any roasted meat, especially leg of lamb. For a better-than-ever rendition of your favorite pumpkin pie recipe, use the cooked pumpkin (without adding the half-and-half, liqueur, and nutmeg) in place of canned pumpkin.

 ELECTRIC COMPATIBLE

MAKES 4 SERVINGS

1 (2-pound) pumpkin, peeled, seeded, and cut into 2-inch chunks

1 1/2 cups water

1/4 cup nonfat half-and-half

1 tablespoon Grand Marnier

1/4 teaspoon ground nutmeg

Place the pumpkin meat in a steamer basket and place basket in a pressure cooker. Add the water. Cover, lock, and bring to high pressure over high heat. Reduce the heat to stabilize pressure and cook for 12 minutes.

Lower the pressure by a quick-release method. Carefully remove the cover. Drain the pumpkin in the strainer, transfer it to a bowl, and mash with a fork. Stir in the half-and-half, liqueur, and nutmeg.

**ROASTING
PEPPERS**

To roast chiles or bell
peppers, cut them in
half and place them,
cut side down, under
the broiler and broil
for 8 to 12 minutes,
turning the peppers
around as they blister
to promote even char-
ring. Remove to a
plastic storage bag for
about 10 minutes to
cool, then rub the
skins off. When dicing
or peeling chiles, wear
rubber gloves to pro-
tect your hands.

Chile Verde Chili

**This colorful chili is indeed green, from the chile peppers to the bell
peppers to the parsley and cilantro. It does boast a generous ration of
pork, but the peppers define its character—the combination of
jalapeño, poblano, and mild green chiles lends the dish a moderately
spicy demeanor that gets hotter as it sits. (Take care not to rub your
eyes after handling hot chiles.) Mayan in derivation, chayote is similar
to summer squash and could be replaced with zucchini if you can't
find it in your market. It has a somewhat bland flavor that tempers the
spiciness of the chile peppers.**

MAKES 6 SERVINGS

1 jalapeño chile, roasted (see below), cored, seeded, deveined,
and chopped (about $\frac{1}{2}$ tablespoon)

1 poblano chile, roasted (see below), cored, seeded, deveined,
and chopped (about $\frac{1}{4}$ cup)

1 mild green chile, roasted (see below), cored, seeded, deveined,
and chopped (about 2 tablespoons)

2 pounds pork loin sirloin, trimmed and cut into $\frac{3}{4}$-inch cubes

1 medium green bell pepper, chopped (about 1 cup)

1 (8-ounce) chayote squash, peeled, seeded, and diced
(about $1\frac{1}{3}$ cups)

8 ounces (about 12) tomatillos, diced (about 1 cup)

1 large white onion, diced (about $1\frac{1}{3}$ cups)

2 cloves garlic, minced, plus 2 additional cloves, peeled

$\frac{3}{4}$ cup Turkey Stock (page 38), defatted Chicken Stock
(page 36 or canned), or water

1 tablespoon dried oregano

2 teaspoons ground cumin

1 teaspoon dried thyme

2 tablespoons chopped fresh cilantro

2 tablespoons chopped fresh parsley

2 tablespoons fresh lime juice

In a pressure cooker, combine the chiles, pork, bell pepper, chayote, tomatillos, onion, and minced garlic. Add the stock, oregano, cumin, and thyme. Cover, lock, and bring to high pressure over high heat. Reduce the heat to stabilize pressure and cook for 25 minutes.

Lower the pressure by a quick-release method. Carefully remove the cover. Stir in the cilantro, parsley, and lime juice and press in the remaining 2 cloves garlic.

Dilled Potatoes

We think this simple, straightforward preparation is the perfect potato for warm summer months when you can't bear the thought of turning on the oven and heating up the kitchen. (We even use it as the basis for a scrumptious potato salad in the variation that follows.) Feel free to substitute other herbs, such as parsley, for the dill. Our recipe yields potatoes retaining just a bit of crunch; if you prefer softer potatoes, cook for 1 minute more.

 ELECTRIC COMPATIBLE

MAKES 4 SERVINGS

7 to 8 small red potatoes (about 1 pound total), scrubbed and quartered

1 cup water

2 tablespoons chopped fresh dill

1 tablespoon unsalted butter

½ teaspoon salt

¼ teaspoon ground black pepper

Put a steamer basket into a pressure cooker and place the potatoes into the basket. Add the water. Cover, lock, and bring to high pressure over high heat. Reduce the heat to stabilize pressure and cook for 3 minutes.

Lower the pressure by a quick-release method. Carefully remove the cover. Drain and transfer the potatoes to a serving bowl. Add the dill, butter, salt, and pepper.

Dilled Potato Salad: Too hot outside to appreciate warm potatoes? No problem. Just substitute ¼ cup reduced-fat mayonnaise for the butter and add a roasted red bell pepper, chopped. Toss to coat, cover, and refrigerate until well chilled.

Horseradish Mashed Potatoes

ELECTRIC COMPATIBLE

These country-style mashed potatoes are slightly chunky, rather than smooth. You could whip them with a sturdy whisk for a smoother texture, but we really prefer the bits of intact potato left by coarsely mashing with a potato masher. Don't drain the potatoes after cooking; the cooking liquid will facilitate mashing and lend added flavor. The potatoes have a tasty but subtle horseradish accent because we start with fresh horseradish and cook it with them. (More balanced than the taste we've experienced in restaurant renditions often flavored by stirring prepared horseradish into already cooked potatoes.) Similarly, adding the garlic to the potatoes before cooking adds a sweetness and mellowness to the garlic.

MAKES 6 SERVINGS

6 medium Yukon Gold potatoes (about 1¾ pounds total), scrubbed and cut into chunks

¾ cup defatted Chicken Stock (page 36 or canned)

⅓ cup grated fresh horseradish root

10 cloves garlic, peeled

2 tablespoons heavy cream

1 tablespoon olive oil

¾ teaspoon salt

¼ teaspoon ground black pepper

Combine the potatoes, stock, and horseradish in a pressure cooker. Press in the garlic cloves. Cover, lock, and bring to high pressure over high heat. Reduce the heat to stabilize pressure and cook for 8 minutes.

Lower the pressure by a quick-release method. Carefully remove the cover. Mash with a potato masher. While continuing to mash, add the cream, oil, salt, and pepper.

Orange-Ginger Sweet Potato Puree

A nice accompaniment to turkey and addition to the Thanksgiving buffet (try it with Roast Turkey with Gravy, page 93), these potatoes have a very creamy consistency. They cook up so soft that you can easily whisk them to a smooth puree. For even fluffier potatoes, use an electric mixer set at medium speed. Look for the crystallized (or candied) ginger—slices of gingerroot that have been boiled in syrup and preserved in cane sugar, often used in baking—in better supermarkets or gourmet stores.

ELECTRIC
COMPATIBLE

MAKES 4 SERVINGS

2 large sweet potatoes (about 2 pounds total), peeled and cut into chunks

$\frac{1}{2}$ cup fresh orange juice

1 tablespoon chopped crystallized ginger

$\frac{1}{2}$ teaspoon ground allspice

2 tablespoons honey

1 tablespoon grated orange zest

$\frac{1}{2}$ teaspoon salt

$\frac{1}{8}$ teaspoon ground black pepper

Combine the sweet potatoes, orange juice, ginger, and allspice in a pressure cooker. Cover, lock, and bring to high pressure over high heat. Reduce the heat to stabilize pressure and cook for 8 minutes.

Lower the pressure by a quick-release method. Carefully remove the cover. Whisk until smooth, then whisk in the honey, orange zest, salt, and pepper. Spoon into a serving bowl.

Grains

Perfect risotto in 7 minutes—with none of the stirring, the incremental additions of stock, or the clean-up mess from multiple pots—is one of the highlights of pressure cooking. We've included enough recipes to keep you in risotto for days, including Red Wine Risotto, a traditional Milanese risotto boasting saffron and beef marrow, sinfully rich Crab Thermidor Risotto, Squash Risotto, and Risotto with Chard. There is even a basic formula to which you can add curried shrimp, smoked chicken or turkey, or just about anything else the that looks good in the pantry.

The better the rice you start with, the better the risotto will be. In addition to Arborio, the starchy, short-grain rice commonly used to make risotto, you might want to try either the Carnaroli or Vialone Nano varieties, which make the creamiest risottos we've ever sampled.

Pressure cooking also does justice to Paella (7 minutes) and to Cajun Jambalaya (10 minutes), as well as to dishes made with barley (15 to 20 minutes). Grits emerge from the cooker creamier than usual; and as with risotto, you'll save considerable stirring. Such typically long-cooking grains as brown rice come off perfect in a fraction of the time.

CAUTION

Because grains can foam quite a bit, take care not to fill your cooker more than about half full. Lower the pressure using the cold water method of release (use the quick-release button on electric models) and rinse the steam valve and the rubber gasket between uses.

Pressure Cooking Times for Grains

All times and proportions in this chart are figured for 1 cup of uncooked grain. Because grains foam quite a bit, fill the pressure cooker only about halfway. If you are cooking the grain by itself, add 1 tablespoon or so of oil to help minimize foaming. Bring the pressure cooker to high pressure, unless otherwise noted. When the grain is done, lower the pressure by the cold water–release method, or with the quick-release button if you are using an electric model. If rice appears to be a bit wet, re-cover the cooker (do not lock it) and allow to sit for 1 to 3 minutes, until the liquid has been absorbed and the rice is fluffy.

Cooking Grains in the Pressure Cooker

1 CUP GRAIN	LIQUID (CUPS)	MINUTES COOKED	YIELD (CUPS)
Barley			
Hulled	$4^1/_2$	18–20	$3^1/_2$
Pearled	$4^1/_2$	15–17	$3^1/_2$
Basmati rice, white	$1^1/_2$	5–7	3
Brown rice	$1^3/_4$	18–20	$2^1/_4$
Grits*	$4^2/_3$	4–5	$5^1/_3$
White rice			
Long-grain	$1^1/_2$	5–6	3
Short-grain, including Arborio, Carnaroli, and Vialone Nano	$2^1/_8$–$2^1/_3$	6–7	3–$3^1/_4$
Wild rice	3	20–22	$2^1/_4$

*Cook grits at low pressure.

Risotto Milanese

Making risotto in a pressure cooker not only eliminates the long, laborious process of stirring in liquid in increments but also guarantees perfect risotto every time—creamy in consistency, but with individual grains of rice still distinct. There's also no need to dirty the second pot in which the stock is kept warm during conventional preparation on the stovetop.

A little of this incredibly rich dish, traditionally served with Osso Buco (page 62), will go a long way. We harvest the marrow from soup bones and freeze it to always have on hand.

ELECTRIC COMPATIBLE *with Revision:*

Use the browning setting to cook the onion and toast the risotto. Lower the pressure using the quick-release button.

MAKES 4 SERVINGS

1 ounce (about 2 tablespoons) beef marrow (optional)

1 tablespoon olive oil

1 small yellow onion, finely chopped (about ¾ cup)

1 cup Arborio rice

2 cups defatted Chicken Stock (page 36 or canned) or Beef Stock (page 41 or canned)

¼ cup dry white wine

⅛ teaspoon crushed saffron threads

⅛ teaspoon ground white pepper

¼ cup freshly grated Parmesan cheese

If using beef marrow, put it into a strainer and hold under hot running water for about 1 minute. Roughly chop.

Heat the oil in a pressure cooker over high heat. Add the onion and marrow, if using. Cook, stirring, until the onion is translucent, about 2 minutes. Add the rice and cook, stirring, for about 30 seconds until the outer edges turn translucent. Add the stock, wine, and saffron. Cover, lock, and bring to high pressure over high heat. Reduce the heat to stabilize pressure and cook for 7 minutes.

Lower the pressure by the cold water–release method. Carefully remove the cover and stir in the white pepper and the cheese. Let sit for 2 minutes before serving.

Risotto Balls

A great way to use up any leftovers; start with well-chilled risotto. Form into balls, using 2 tablespoons for each, and spray lightly with olive oil. Cook in a preheated nonstick skillet over medium-high heat until well browned all over, 10 to 12 minutes, turning for even browning.

Red Wine Risotto

ELECTRIC COMPATIBLE *with Revision:*

Use the browning setting to cook the onion and toast the rice. Lower the pressure using the quick-release button.

Risotto can easily be a meal in itself. As a side dish for six, this risotto pairs nicely with beef or a full-flavored fish, such as grilled tuna. Piedmontese in origin, Red Wine Risotto was originally made with barolo, but as that wine has gotten rather pricy of late any good red will do. As with all risottos—all grain dishes, for that matter—let the rice sit for a couple of minutes before serving. For an even creamier risotto, stir in 1 or 2 tablespoons of butter just before you serve it.

MAKES 4 SERVINGS

1 tablespoon unsalted butter

1 tablespoon olive oil

1 small yellow onion, chopped (about ½ cup)

1 cup Arborio rice

4 ounces white button mushrooms, cleaned, stemmed, and thinly sliced (about 1 cup)

1¾ cups defatted Chicken Stock (page 36 or canned) or water

½ cup dry red wine

⅛ teaspoon ground black pepper

2 tablespoons freshly grated Parmesan cheese

Combine the butter and oil in a pressure cooker. Warm over high heat just until the mixture begins to give off steam. Add the onion and cook, stirring constantly, until translucent, about 2 minutes. Add the rice and cook, stirring, until it is thoroughly coated, about 30 seconds. Stir in the mushrooms, stock or water, wine, and pepper. Cover, lock, and bring to high pressure over high heat. Reduce the heat to stabilize pressure and cook for 7 minutes.

Lower the pressure by the cold water–release method. Carefully remove the cover and stir in the cheese. Let sit for 2 minutes before serving.

Squash Risotto

Our favorite risotto, this dish also could serve six as a side. Preparation of the recipe without the pressure cooker would take three pots—one each for the rice, stock, and squash. The basil stirred in at the end contrasts nicely with the sweetness of the squash.

 ELECTRIC COMPATIBLE *with Revision:*

Use the browning setting to cook the onion and toast the rice. Lower the pressure using the quick-release button.

MAKES 4 SERVINGS

¹⁄₂ tablespoon olive oil

1 green onion, trimmed to white and light green parts and chopped (about 2 tablespoons)

1 cup Arborio rice

9 ounces butternut squash, peeled, seeded, and cut into ¹⁄₂-inch cubes (about 1¹⁄₃ cups)

2 cups defatted Chicken Stock (page 36 or canned) or water

¹⁄₄ cup dry white wine

¹⁄₂ teaspoon ground nutmeg

1 tablespoon chopped fresh basil

2 tablespoons freshly grated Parmesan cheese

Salt to taste

Ground black pepper to taste

Combine the oil and green onion in a pressure cooker over medium heat. Cook, stirring, just until the onion begins to wilt, about 2 minutes. Add the rice and cook, stirring constantly, until thoroughly coated, about 1 minute. Stir in the squash, stock or water, wine, and nutmeg. Cover, lock, and bring to high pressure over high heat. Reduce the heat to stabilize pressure and cook for 7 minutes.

Lower the pressure by the cold water–release method. Carefully remove the cover and stir in the basil, cheese, salt, and pepper. Let sit for 2 minutes before serving.

Crab Thermidor Risotto

We hit on this winning formula, which could also serve six as a first course, one New Year's Eve in Duck, North Carolina, when all the lobsters at the supermarket had been spoken for by the time we arrived. Should you have any leftovers, which is possible but hardly likely, make them into Risotto Balls (page 146) the next day.

MAKES 4 SERVINGS

1 tablespoon olive oil

1 large shallot, minced (about $\frac{1}{2}$ cup)

$1\frac{1}{4}$ cups Arborio rice

4 ounces white button mushrooms, cleaned, stemmed, and chopped (about $1\frac{1}{4}$ cups)

$1\frac{1}{2}$ cups clam juice

$1\frac{1}{4}$ cups defatted Chicken Stock (page 36 or canned)

3 tablespoons sherry

1 teaspoon Worcestershire sauce

1 pound lump crabmeat, picked over

2 tablespoons grated Parmesan cheese

$\frac{1}{2}$ teaspoon salt

$\frac{1}{8}$ teaspoon ground black pepper

Chopped fresh parsley for garnish

ELECTRIC COMPATIBLE

with Revision:

Use the browning setting to cook the shallot, toast the rice, and bring the mixture to a gentle boil. Lower the pressure using the quick-release button.

Combine the oil and shallot in a pressure cooker over medium heat. Cook, stirring constantly, until the shallot is just beginning to turn golden, about 4 minutes. Add the rice and cook, stirring constantly, until the outer edges turn translucent, about 1 minute. Stir in the mushrooms, clam juice, and stock. Bring to a boil over high heat, stirring occasionally. Add 2 tablespoons of the sherry and the Worcestershire sauce. Cover, lock, and bring to high pressure over high heat. Reduce the heat to stabilize pressure and cook for 7 minutes.

Lower the pressure by the cold water–release method. Carefully remove the cover. Stir in the crabmeat, Parmesan cheese, salt, pepper, and the remaining 1 tablespoon sherry. Serve, garnished with the parsley.

Risotto with Chard

You could also use green chard, kale, or escarole in this side dish, but we rather like the slight ruby tint lent by red chard, also called rhubarb chard, which has a stronger flavor than green chard as well. The addition of a bit of goat cheese in place of the typical Parmesan lends a very smooth, rich texture.

MAKES 6 SERVINGS

6 ounces red chard

1 small yellow onion, diced (about ¾ cup)

1 cup Arborio rice

2 cups defatted Beef Stock (page 41 or canned)

3 tablespoons dry white wine

2 ounces creamy goat cheese (such as Montrachet)

¼ teaspoon salt

⅛ teaspoon ground black pepper

Stem the chard. Chop the stems (about ½ cup) and the leaves (about 1¼ packed cups).

Preheat a pressure cooker over medium-high heat. Add the chard

ELECTRIC
COMPATIBLE
with Revision:

Use the the browning setting to cook the chard stems and onion and toast the rice. Lower the pressure using the quick-release button.

stems and onion and cook until the stems are very soft, about 2 minutes. Add the rice and cook, stirring constantly, until the outer shells are translucent, about 1 minute. Stir in the stock and wine. Cover, lock, and bring to high pressure over high heat. Reduce the heat to stabilize pressure and cook for 7 minutes.

Lower the pressure by the cold water–release method. Carefully remove the cover. Stir in the chard leaves, goat cheese, salt, and pepper. Let sit for 1 minute before serving.

Mix and Match Risotto

This is a versatile basic formula for perfect risotto made painless in the pressure cooker. Start with Arborio rice or—for even better risotto—Vialone Nano or Carnaroli rice (also imported from Italy) or an interesting new American strain called Cal Riso. Served plain or with one of our suggested finishes (see variations, below), the recipe makes enough for entertaining or for two generous main-course portions.

MAKES 4 SERVINGS

1/2 tablespoon olive oil

1 large shallot, chopped (about 1/3 cup)

1 cup Arborio rice

2 cups defatted Chicken Stock (page 36 or canned)

3 tablespoons dry white wine

Preheat a pressure cooker over medium-high heat. Swirl in the oil, then sauté the shallot in the oil until it is very soft, about 2 minutes. Add the rice and cook, stirring constantly, until the outer shells are translucent, about 1 minute. Stir in the stock and wine. Cover, lock, and bring to high pressure over high heat. Reduce the heat to stabilize pressure and cook for 7 minutes.

Lower the pressure by the cold water–release method. Carefully remove the cover.

VARIATIONS

Finishing Your Risotto with a Flourish: **After the pressure has been lowered, carefully remove the cover from the cooker and stir in one of the following combinations.**

12 ounces cooked peeled shrimp, cut in half

$1/2$ tablespoon Curry Powder (page 32 or purchased)

1 tablespoon unsalted butter

6 ounces smoked chicken, chopped

1 teaspoon dried thyme or 1 tablespoon fresh thyme

$1/4$ cup chopped fresh parsley

3 tablespoons freshly grated Parmesan cheese

1 cup frozen green peas, thawed

8 ounces smoked turkey sausage, roughly chopped

1 tablespoon unsalted butter

$1^1/2$ tablespoons freshly grated Parmesan cheese

Cajun Jambalaya

Beyond the basic elements of rice and Louisiana spicing, jambalayas can include any of a variety of meats and seafood. Our version is brimming with sausage, chicken, and shrimp, spiked with a bit of Creole seasoning that makes it slightly spicier than typical. Choose any spicy smoked sausage; we usually use smoked turkey sausage, which helps keep the dish on the lean side.

MAKES 4 SERVINGS

ELECTRIC
COMPATIBLE
with Revision:

Cook at high pressure for 7 minutes if your cooker works only at high pressure.

1 medium yellow onion, chopped (about 1 cup)

1 medium green bell pepper, chopped (about 1 cup)

3 cloves garlic, minced

1 (14½-ounce) can diced tomatoes

4 ounces smoked turkey sausage, sliced

1 pound medium shrimp, peeled and deveined

1 (6-ounce) skinless, boneless chicken breast, cubed

½ cup long-grain white rice

1 cup defatted Chicken Stock (page 36 or canned)

½ tablespoon Creole Seasoning (page 77 or purchased)

½ teaspoon dried thyme

⅛ teaspoon cayenne pepper

Combine all ingredients in a pressure cooker. Stir to mix. Cover, lock, and bring to low pressure over high heat. Reduce the heat to stabilize pressure and cook for 10 minutes. (If your machine will only work at high pressure, cook for 7 minutes.)

Remove the pressure cooker from the heat and let the pressure drop naturally. Carefully remove the cover. Let sit until all liquid has been absorbed.

Paella

ELECTRIC
COMPATIBLE
with Revision:

Use the browning setting for all the initial cooking steps before the cooker is covered and sealed. Lower the pressure using the quick-release button.

Named after the wide, shallow pan in which it is traditionally cooked, paella is a passion throughout much of the Spanish-speaking world. Although Spaniards claim it as a national resource of sorts, some of the best we've had have been served up in South America. We prefer to make it with fragrant long-grain basmati rice, which is Indian and Pakistani in origin. Basmati used to be expensive and require extensive washing, much like wild rice; but it has come to be readily available in supermarkets in recent years and no longer requires any special cleaning. Use the largest littleneck clams (sometimes called

topnecks on the East Coast) you can find. For this lean dish, much of the fat is rendered from the chicken as it browns and is then poured off.

MAKES 6 SERVINGS

1 tablespoon olive oil

8 ounces spicy country-style or hot Italian sausage, pricked with the tines of a fork

4 (7-ounce) chicken thighs, visible fat removed

1 large yellow onion, chopped (about 1½ cups)

1 large stalk celery, chopped (about ½ cup)

1 small green bell pepper, chopped (about ¾ cup)

3 cloves garlic, minced

1¾ cups Fish Stock (page 40 or frozen) or clam juice

¼ cup dry white wine

12 large littleneck clams in shells, scrubbed

2 plum tomatoes, seeded and chopped (about 1 cup)

1⅓ cups white basmati rice

8 ounces medium shrimp, peeled and deveined

¼ teaspoon dried thyme

¼ teaspoon cayenne pepper

¼ teaspoon crushed saffron threads

2 tablespoons chopped fresh parsley

Preheat a pressure cooker over medium-low heat. Increase the heat to medium and swirl in the oil to coat the bottom. Add the sausage and cook until browned all over, about 10 minutes, turning as needed. Remove the sausage from the cooker, cut into ½-inch pieces, and set aside.

Put the chicken into the cooker, skin side down, and cook over medium heat until browned, about 5 minutes. Turn over and brown the other side, about 5 minutes. Remove the chicken to a plate and discard the drippings from the cooker. Add the onion, celery, bell pepper, and garlic and cook, stirring constantly, until the vegetables soften, about 1 minute. Add the stock or juice and the wine and bring to a boil. Add the clams. Cover (do not seal) and cook until the clams open, about 5 minutes. Remove the clams to a bowl with a slotted spoon, discarding any that do not open, and cover with foil to keep warm.

Add the tomatoes, rice, shrimp, thyme, cayenne, and saffron to the cooker. Return the sausage and the chicken. Cover, seal, and bring to high pressure over high heat. Reduce the heat to stabilize pressure and cook for 7 minutes.

Lower the pressure by the cold water–release method. Carefully remove the cover. Return the clams to the cooker. Cover (do not seal) and set aside for 3 minutes. Remove the clams and chicken to a serving platter. Stir the remaining mixture and mound alongside. Garnish with the parsley.

ELECTRIC
COMPATIBLE
with Revision:

Lower the pressure using the quick-release button.

Barley with Mushrooms

Barley stands in for Arborio rice in this risotto-like dish. Because we start with pearled barley and finish the dish with a generous addition of Parmesan cheese, it has a much creamier consistency than our Barley and Field Peas (page 155). It can serve as a first course for four as well a good accompaniment to broiled or grilled meats.

MAKES 6 SERVINGS

4 medium green onions, trimmed to white and light green parts and chopped (about ½ cup)

1 cup pearled barley

2½ cups defatted Beef Stock (page 41 or canned)

4 ounces white button mushrooms, cleaned, stemmed, and chopped (about 1 cup)

⅛ teaspoon ground black pepper

3 tablespoons freshly grated Parmesan cheese

Combine the green onions, barley, stock, and mushrooms in a pressure cooker. Cover, lock, and bring to high pressure over high heat. Reduce the heat to stabilize pressure and cook for 15 minutes.

Lower the pressure by the cold water–release method. Carefully remove the cover and stir in the pepper and cheese.

Barley and Field Peas

We've adapted a Czech specialty from the late Bert Greene for this hearty side dish, in which the softness of the barley is juxtaposed with the slightly crunchy field peas. Either dried lentils or dried green peas can be substituted for field peas, which are basically split peas that have not been split—but don't use split peas, because they would turn to mush in the pressure cooker. Hulled barley, the most nutritious form, has had only the outer husk removed, not the bran as pearled barley does.

ELECTRIC
COMPATIBLE
with Revision:

Lower the pressure using the quick-release button.

MAKES 6 SERVINGS

4 ounces country-style ham, trimmed and chopped

1 cup hulled barley (not pearled), rinsed

1 cup field peas, rinsed

1 medium yellow onion, finely chopped (about 1 cup)

3½ cups defatted Chicken Stock (page 36 or canned)

½ teaspoon dried sage

¼ teaspoon dried oregano

⅛ teaspoon ground black pepper

Combine the ham, barley, field peas, onion, stock, sage, and oregano in a pressure cooker. Cover, lock, and bring to high pressure over high heat. Reduce the heat to stabilize pressure and cook for 18 minutes.

Lower the pressure by the cold water–release method. Carefully remove the cover, and stir in the pepper.

ELECTRIC
COMPATIBLE
with Revision:

*Compatible only if your
cooker works at low
pressure. Use the browning
setting to bring the water
to a gentle boil.*

Ham and Cheese Grits

**Serve this filling dish, which brings together down-home country ham
and upscale Montrachet goat cheese, for breakfast or on the side; but
use long-cooking grits, not the instant or quick-cooking variety. Making the dish in the pressure cooker eliminates the need to stir fre-
quently and yields smoother, creamier grits. Because they could easily
burn with too much heat, grits are not a good candidate for making in
a cooker that works only on high pressure.**

MAKES 4 SERVINGS

3½ cups water

1 shallot, minced (about ¼ cup)

1 clove garlic, minced

¾ cup old-fashioned grits

4 ounces country-style ham, chopped

2 ounces creamy goat cheese (such as Montrachet)

½ teaspoon salt

¼ teaspoon ground black pepper

Combine the water, shallot, and garlic in a pressure cooker. Bring to a
boil over high heat. Stir in the grits and ham and reduce the heat to
medium-low. Cover, lock, and bring to low pressure over medium-low
heat. Adjust the heat as necessary to stabilize pressure. Cook for 4
minutes.

Lower the pressure by the cold water–release method. Carefully
remove the cover. Whisk to blend. Whisk in the goat cheese, salt, and
pepper. Let sit for 1 minute, then serve immediately.

Brown Rice and Clams

When eating this treat, Barry likes to close his eyes and transport himself back to childhood and a similar dish served up at a little clam shack on Falmouth Pier. A filling main course for four, Brown Rice and Clams works nicely as a side for six with Fish Stew (page 109). Made into a pie (see variation below), it is a great luncheon dish augmented by only a salad and perhaps a very dry and well-chilled white wine. If you wish to use fresh clams, you'll need ²/₃ cup chopped clams, plus 1¹/₂ cups clam juice or 1 cup clam juice and ¹/₂ cup water. The dish can also be made with white rice, which is the more traditional rendition.

ELECTRIC COMPATIBLE *with Revision:*

Use the browning setting to cook the onion and garlic. Lower the pressure using the quick-release button.

MAKES 4 SERVINGS

    2 (6¹/₂-ounce) cans chopped clams

    1 tablespoon unsalted butter

    1 medium yellow onion, chopped (about 1 cup)

    1 large clove garlic, minced

    1 cup long-grain brown rice

    1 teaspoon chopped jalapeño chile

    About ¹/₂ cup water

    2 teaspoons freshly grated Parmesan cheese

    ¹/₄ teaspoon dried thyme or ³/₄ teaspoon fresh thyme

    ¹/₄ teaspoon salt

    ¹/₈ teaspoon ground white pepper

Drain the clams, reserving their juice.

Melt the butter in a pressure cooker over medium heat. Add the onion and garlic. Cook, stirring constantly, until the onion is translucent, about 2 minutes. Stir in the rice and jalapeño. Add sufficient water to the reserved clam juice to make 1¹/₂ cups and stir it into the cooker. Cover, lock, and bring to high pressure over high heat. Reduce the heat to stabilize pressure and cook for 18 minutes.

Lower the pressure by the cold water–release method. Carefully remove the cover. Stir in the clams, Parmesan cheese, and thyme. Cover (do not lock) the cooker and let sit off the heat for 5 minutes. Stir in the salt and white pepper.

VARIATION

New England Clam Pie: Preheat the oven to 350F (175C). Line a pie plate with an unbaked 9-inch pie crust. Prick all over with the tines of a fork and bake for 5 minutes. Break 2 large eggs into the rice and clam mixture. Add ⅓ cup half-and-half and stir to mix. Scoop into the shell, cover with thin slices of provolone cheese, and bake until the cheese has melted and lightly browned, 25 to 30 minutes.

Beans

Like many folks, we used to ignore dried beans—as nutritious and good as they are—when planning everyday meals because they just take too long to prepare by conventional cooking methods. The pressure cooker has restored beans in all their glory to our workday diets—from White Bean Stew (which is also the base for one pretty terrific cassoulet) to Appaloosa Bean Ragoût, Cajun Red Beans and Rice to Barbecue Beans. All of these dishes can now be made in 20 or 30 minutes from start to finish in the pressure cooker.

Not only will the cooker cook your beans quickly, it will also eliminate the need to soak beans for an extended period of time first to promote faster and more even cooking. Just combine the beans with water in the pressure cooker and cook for 2 to 3 minutes at high pressure as the first step in most bean recipes.

We've also rediscovered chilis, equally quickly prepared in the cooker and great for making in quantity for parties and lazy weekend noshes. Try our recipes for Spicy Black Bean Chili (28 minutes), White Chili made with navy beans and turkey (18 minutes), and Adobo Pinto Bean and Pork Chili (23 minutes).

CAUTION

Because beans foam quite a bit, you should fill the pressure cooker only about halfway. Rinse the steam valve and the rubber gasket between uses.

Beans are one of the more inconsistent of foods when it comes to cooking times. These estimates are based on our own experience; should you find the beans done a little less than to your liking, re-lock the cooker, bring it back to pressure, and cook for 1 to 3 minutes more to the desired doneness.

About 1 cup dried beans will yield 2 to 2½ cups cooked beans. To the beans, add at least the minimum amount of liquid recommended for cooking beans by your pressure cooker's manufacturer (the amount needed will vary for different models). Never add salt before pressure cooking, as it would toughen the beans' outer shells. When the beans are done, remove the cooker from the heat and allow the pressure to drop naturally.

We have given times for pressure cooking both soaked and unsoaked beans. If you are going to incorporate the beans in a recipe, we recommend soaking them first as they will need to cook a bit more than most other ingredients and soaking reduces cooking time. Soaking also facilitates more even cooking. There are three methods for soaking beans. You can soak them overnight in cold water. You can boil them for 5 minutes on the stovetop, remove the pan from the heat, cover it, and let the beans sit for 1 hour. Or, easiest of all, you can "soak" beans by pressure cooking. Add 4 cups of water to the pressure cooker for every 1 cup of beans, cover, lock, bring to high pressure over high heat, reduce the heat to stabilize pressure, and cook for 3 minutes; lower the pressure using the cold water–release method or, with an electric cooker, using the quick-release button.

Remember that beans foam quite a bit. Fill the pressure cooker only about halfway, and add a tablespoon or so of oil to help minimize foaming if you are cooking the beans by themselves.

Cooking Dried Beans in the Pressure Cooker

BEANS	MINUTES AT HIGH PRESSURE, SOAKED BEANS	MINUTES AT HIGH PRESSURE, UNSOAKED BEANS
Adzuki	6–8	15–17
Ansazi	5–7	13–15
Appaloosa, red or black	11–13	22–25
Black (turtle)	10–12	22–25
Black-eyed peas	No soaking required	10–12
Calypso	5–7	12–15
Cannellini	11–13	24–27
Chickpeas (garbanzos)		
Whole	10–12	25–27
Split baby	No soaking required	4–6
Cranberry	10–12	24–26
Fava	14–16	25–27
Field peas	No soaking required	17–19
Flageolet	11–13	18–20
Great Northern	9–11	24–26
Green peas	No soaking required	17–20
Kidney, red	11–13	22–26
Lentils		
Brown, green, or red	No soaking required	8–10 (crunchy for salads)
		10–12 (softer for soups)
Black Beluga	No soaking required	5–7
Lima (butter)	4–6	13–15
Navy	7–9	15–18
Pigeon	6–8	18–22
Pink	9–11	22–24
Pinto	8–10	20–22
Red nightfall	11–14	28–30
Scarlet runner	10–12	18–20
Soybeans	10–12	27–30
Split peas, green or yellow	No soaking required	10–12
Tiger eye	11–14	28–30

ELECTRIC
COMPATIBLE
with Revision:

Use the browning setting to bring the water and beans to a gentle boil. Lower the pressure using the quick-release button.

White Bean Stew

The primary ingredient in Cassoulet (opposite), this robust stew is sort of a down-and-dirty cassoulet on its own—a satisfying meal paired with a salad, a hunk of bread, and a glass of wine.

MAKES 8 SERVINGS

3½ cups dried Great Northern beans, picked over

14 cups water

8 sprigs fresh thyme

8 sprigs fresh parsley

2 bay leaves

1½ pounds pork loin sirloin, trimmed and cut into chunks

1½ pounds veal leg or shoulder stew meat, trimmed and cut into chunks

1 large onion, diced (about 1½ cups)

1 large stalk celery, diced (about ½ cup)

1 large carrot, peeled and diced (about ½ cup)

8 cloves garlic, minced

4 cups Duck Stock (page 39) or defatted Chicken Stock (page 36 or canned)

Combine the beans and water in a pressure cooker over high heat. Bring to a full boil. Cover, lock, and bring to high pressure. Reduce the heat to stabilize pressure and cook for 3 minutes.

Lower the pressure using the cold water–release method and carefully remove the cover. Drain and return the beans to the cooker. Tie the thyme, parsley, and bay leaves together to make a bouquet garni and add it to the cooker, along with the remaining ingredients. Cover, lock, and bring back to high pressure over high heat. Reduce the heat to stabilize pressure and cook for 20 minutes.

Lower the pressure by the cold water–release method. Carefully remove the cover.

Cassoulet

It *is* a lot of work, but cassoulet is one of those magnificent dishes that just naturally generate the oohs and aahs that make it all worthwhile. It was our dish of choice last Christmas Eve, the once-a-year meal for which we pull out all stops. If you have dinner guests who, like one of ours, don't particularly care for lamb, make the Cassoulet, or at least a portion of it, with the tomato and rosemary substitution. This recipe produces a huge yield and is very, very rich—it's a dish that can really feed an army.

MAKES 20 SERVINGS

1 recipe Duck Confit (page 87)

1 recipe White Bean Stew (opposite)

4 large cloves garlic, minced (about 2 tablespoons)

1 pound andouille sausage, roughly chopped

1 recipe Lamb Ragoût (page 178) or 1 (14½-ounce) can diced tomatoes and 2 tablespoons chopped fresh rosemary

5 to 6 cups Duck Stock (page 39) or defatted Chicken Stock (page 36 or canned)

1½ cups plain breadcrumbs

¼ cup chopped fresh parsley

Preheat the oven to 325F (165C).

Remove the duck from the confit, skin it, and bone the thighs and drumsticks. Roughly chop the meat.

Put half the bean stew into the bottom of an ovenproof 5-quart casserole. Scatter about 2 teaspoons of the garlic over the beans. Add all of the duck in a layer, then the sausage. Add the lamb in a layer (if using the tomatoes, sprinkle with the rosemary). Scatter another 2 teaspoons of garlic over this layer. Add the remaining bean stew, scatter the remaining 2 teaspoons garlic, and pour in enough stock to come to the top of the beans. Top with a layer of breadcrumbs and parsley.

Bake for 30 minutes. Stir the crusty top into the casserole and bake for 30 minutes more. The cassoulet should be a bit wet and bubbling. If it looks very dry, add enough stock to come to the top of the beans and set aside for about 5 minutes for the stock to be absorbed.

Spicy Barbecue Beans

**We like this side dish best rewarmed a day after it's made, when it
has a firmer consistency than it does right out of the cooker—warm in
a preheated 350F (175C) oven for 30 minutes. Be sure to rinse and
dry the pressure cooker before starting the second step; cooking the
bacon will cause any residual moisture to spatter. If you can't find a
banana chile—a long, thin chile somewhat milder than a jalapeño, substitute a chopped jalapeño.**

MAKES 8 SERVINGS

1$\frac{1}{3}$ cups dried Great Northern beans, picked over

5$\frac{1}{2}$ cups water

3 slices bacon, diced

1 medium yellow onion, diced (about 1 cup)

1 medium yellow banana chile, cored, seeded, deveined, and
chopped (about 2 tablespoons)

12 ounces ale

1 (8-ounce) can tomato sauce

$\frac{1}{4}$ cup dark molasses

2 tablespoons red wine vinegar

$\frac{1}{2}$ tablespoon Worcestershire sauce

1 teaspoon hickory Liquid Smoke

1 tablespoon dry mustard

1 tablespoon packed dark brown sugar

Combine the beans and the water in a pressure cooker over high
heat. Bring to a boil. Cover, lock, and bring to high pressure over
high heat. Reduce the heat to stabilize pressure and cook for 10 minutes.

Remove the pressure cooker from the heat and let the pressure
drop naturally. Carefully remove the cover. Drain the beans and set
them aside. Rinse and dry the cooker.

Cook the bacon in the pressure cooker over medium heat just until it gives off fat, about 5 minutes. Add the onion and chile and cook, stirring constantly, until the onion begins to color, about 3 minutes. Stir in the ale, tomato sauce, molasses, vinegar, Worcestershire sauce, Liquid Smoke, dry mustard, and brown sugar. Return the beans to the cooker, cover, lock, and bring to high pressure over high heat. Reduce the heat to stabilize pressure and cook for 15 minutes.

Remove the cooker from the heat and let the pressure drop naturally. Carefully remove the cover.

Black Beans with Onion

Pair these hearty beans, which are much thicker than the traditional Cuban black beans, with Chile Verde Chili (page 138) for a filling meal.

ELECTRIC
COMPATIBLE
with Revision:

Use the browning setting to bring the water to a gentle boil. Lower the pressure using the quick-release button.

MAKES 6 SERVINGS

    1 cup dried black beans, picked over

    1 small white onion, peeled

    1 whole red finger chile

    1 bay leaf

    2 large cloves garlic, peeled

    5½ cups water

    1 medium yellow onion, diced (about 1 cup)

    ¼ cup tomato sauce

    1 tablespoon sun-dried tomato paste

    ½ tablespoon ground cumin

    1 teaspoon ground coriander

    2 tablespoons chopped fresh cilantro

Combine the beans, white onion, chile, bay leaf, 1 clove of garlic, and

5 cups of the water in a pressure cooker. Bring to a boil over high heat. Cover, lock, and bring to high pressure over high heat. Reduce the heat to stabilize pressure and cook for 15 minutes.

Lower the pressure by the cold water–release method. Carefully remove the cover. Drain the beans, removing and discarding the whole onion, garlic clove, chile, and bay leaf, and return the beans to the cooker. Add the yellow onion, tomato sauce, tomato paste, cumin, coriander, and the remaining ½ cup water. Cover, lock, and bring to high pressure over high heat. Reduce the heat to stabilize pressure and cook for 5 minutes.

Lower the pressure by the cold water–release method. Carefully remove the cover. Let sit for 10 minutes. Before serving, mince and stir in the remaining garlic clove or press it in. Serve, garnished with the cilantro.

Cajun Red Beans and Rice

Pass hot sauce on the side when you serve this N'awlins specialty, which could also serve four as a main course. Any smoked sausage will do, from the traditional Louisiana andouille to smoked turkey sausage if you're watching fat grams.

MAKES 6 SERVINGS

    1 cup dried red kidney beans, picked over

    5 cups water

    1 medium yellow onion, chopped (about 1 cup)

    2 large cloves garlic, minced

    1 small green bell pepper, chopped (about ¾ cup)

    1 teaspoon chopped jalapeño chile

    ¾ cup long-grain white rice

    4 ounces smoked sausage, diced

    ¾ teaspoon dried thyme

    ¼ teaspoon ground black pepper

ELECTRIC
COMPATIBLE
with Revision:

Use the browning setting to bring the beans and water to a gentle boil. Lower the pressure using the quick-release button.

2 bay leaves

2 cups Smoked Turkey Stock (page 38) or defatted Chicken Stock (page 36 or canned)

½ teaspoon salt

Combine the kidney beans and water in a pressure cooker and bring to a boil over high heat. Cover, lock, and bring to high pressure. Reduce the heat to stabilize pressure and cook for 3 minutes.

Lower the pressure by the cold water–release method. Carefully remove the cover. Drain the beans, rinse, and return them to the cooker. Add the onion, garlic, bell pepper, jalapeño, rice, sausage, thyme, black pepper, bay leaves, and stock. Bring to a boil over high heat. Cover, lock, and bring to high pressure over high heat. Reduce the heat to stabilize pressure and cook for 9 minutes.

Lower the pressure by the cold water–release method. Carefully remove the cover and set aside for about 1 minute to allow all liquid to be absorbed. Discard the bay leaves, stir in the salt, and serve.

VARIATION

Dirty Rice: For Cajun dirty rice, omit the beans and water, skip the first step, and add 1 pound chicken livers, chopped, or ½ pound each liver and gizzards, chopped, along with the other ingredients and pressure cook as directed.

ELECTRIC
COMPATIBLE
with Revision:

Cook on high pressure for
16 minutes if your cooker
only works at high
pressure.

Black-Eyed Peas

**Throughout the South, it's a New Year's tradition to serve black-eyed
peas, which are native to Africa and also called cow peas, for good
luck. In the Carolina Low Country, the dish would be paired with a
pot of rice to make hoppin' John; it's also quite good with cornbread.
Look for the ham hock with other smoked meats in your supermarket's meat counter. The long, thin red finger chile (you could also use
2 small red serrano chiles) is very spicy and adds flavor even though
used whole and discarded before serving.**

MAKES 4 SERVINGS

1½ cups dried black-eyed peas, picked over

1 smoked ham hock

1 small yellow onion, chopped (about ½ cup)

2 small stalks celery, chopped (about ½ cup)

2 small carrots, peeled and chopped (about ⅓ cup)

1 red finger chile pepper

12 ounces beer

1 cup vegetable stock or water

½ cup chopped red bell pepper

2 tablespoons chopped fresh parsley

2 cloves garlic, minced

½ tablespoon Worcestershire sauce

¼ teaspoon green hot sauce

½ teaspoon salt

¼ teaspoon ground black pepper

Combine the black-eyed peas, ham hock, onion, celery, carrots, chile,
beer, and stock or water in a pressure cooker. Cover, lock, and bring to
low pressure over high heat. Reduce the heat to stabilize pressure and
cook for 20 minutes. (If your pressure cooker will only work at high
pressure, cook for 16 minutes.)

Remove the pressure cooker from the heat and let the pressure
drop naturally. Carefully remove the cover. Remove and discard the

chile. Remove the ham hock, discard the skin, and chop the meat and return it to the cooker. Stir in the bell pepper, parsley, garlic, Worcestershire sauce, hot sauce, salt, and black pepper.

Adobo Pinto Bean and Pork Chili

Be sure to drain and reserve the adobo tomato sauce in which the chipotles are packed. The chiles and their juice lend this New Mexican dish a character as fiery as the desert in which it originated. It's often served with white rice, which tames it down a bit.

ELECTRIC COMPATIBLE
with Revision:

Use the browning setting to bring the water and beans to a gentle boil and to warm the pork mixture until steamy. Lower the pressure using the quick-release button.

MAKES 6 TO 8 SERVINGS

2 cups dried pinto beans, picked over

8 cups water

1 pound pork loin sirloin, trimmed and diced

3 canned chipotle chiles, cored, seeded, deveined, and chopped (about 2 generous tablespoons) plus ¼ cup sauce from the can

2 medium stalks celery, diced (about ¾ cup)

1 small white onion, diced (about ¾ cup)

1 (28-ounce) can crushed tomatoes in puree

1 tablespoon sugar

1 teaspoon ground cumin

½ teaspoon ground coriander

1 cup dry red wine

3 tablespoons chopped fresh cilantro

1 tablespoon red wine vinegar

Combine the beans and the water in a pressure cooker over high heat; bring to a boil. Cover, lock, and bring to high pressure over high heat. Reduce the heat to stabilize pressure and cook for 3 minutes.

Lower the pressure by the cold water–release method. Carefully remove the cover. Drain the beans and return them to the cooker. Add the pork, chiles and sauce, celery, onion, tomatoes, sugar, cumin, coriander, and wine. While stirring, warm over high heat until the mixture begins to steam. Cover, lock, and bring to high pressure over high heat. Reduce the heat to stabilize the pressure and cook for 20 minutes.

Lower the pressure by the cold water–release method. Carefully remove the cover and stir in the cilantro and vinegar.

White Chili

ELECTRIC COMPATIBLE *with Revision:*

Use the browning setting to bring the water and beans to a gentle boil. Lower the pressure using the quick-release button.

Also known as Pasilla peppers, or ancho chiles when they are dried, poblanos are plump, dark green, and fairly hot. They are used extensively in Mexico, the basis of chiles rellenos. They add flavor and a bit of color to this otherwise monochromatic dish (white beans, turkey, and white pepper). We sometimes sprinkle servings with grated jalapeño Monterey Jack cheese.

MAKES 6 SERVINGS

1½ cups dried navy beans, picked over

6 cups water

1 tablespoon olive oil

1 pound turkey breast tenderloin, cut into bite-sized pieces

2 large stalks celery, chopped (about 1 cup)

1 medium yellow onion, chopped (about 1 cup)

2 poblano chiles, roasted (see page 138 for roasting directions), cored, seeded, deveined, and chopped (about ½ cup)

1 large jalapeño chile, cored, seeded, deveined, and minced (about 2 tablespoons)

1 tablespoon ground cumin

1 tablespoon dried oregano

2 cups Smoked Turkey Stock (page 38), Turkey Stock (page 38), or defatted Chicken Stock (page 36 or canned)

3 cloves garlic, peeled

1/3 cup chopped fresh cilantro

1/2 teaspoon green hot sauce or to taste

1/2 teaspoon salt

1/4 teaspoon ground white pepper

Combine the beans and the water in a pressure cooker. Bring to a boil over high heat. Cover, lock, and bring to high pressure. Reduce the heat to stabilize pressure and cook for 3 minutes.

Lower the pressure by the cold water–release method. Carefully remove the cover. Drain and set aside the beans. Rinse and dry the cooker and add the oil. Warm over high heat. Add the turkey, celery, and onion. Cook, stirring constantly, until the turkey is no longer pink, about 3 minutes. Stir in the chiles, cumin, and oregano. Add the stock and return the beans to the cooker. Cover, lock, and bring to high pressure over high heat. Reduce the heat to stabilize pressure and cook for 15 minutes.

Lower the pressure by the cold water–release method. Carefully remove the cover and press in the garlic. Stir in the cilantro, hot sauce, salt, and ground pepper and serve.

Spicy Black Bean Chili

An Anaheim chile (the long, lime-green pepper with a pointy tip, also known as a California long green or a New Mexico chile) lends full-flavor heat to this complex, earthy dish, along with hot paprika. It's the kind of thick, hearty, and traditionally long-cooking dish that Barry used to spend all day preparing before he discovered the pressure cooker. Serve with extra onion and chopped jalapeño on the side.

MAKES 6 SERVINGS

ELECTRIC
COMPATIBLE
with Revision:

Use the browning setting to bring the water and beans to a gentle boil. Lower the pressure using the quick-release button.

1⅓ cups dried black beans, picked over

5 cups water

1 (14½-ounce) can diced tomatoes

1 medium yellow onion, diced (about 1 cup)

1 Anaheim chile, cored, seeded, deveined, and chopped (about ⅓ cup)

4 ounces ham steak, trimmed and diced

2 tablespoons chili powder

1 tablespoon ground cumin

1 tablespoon dried oregano, crushed

1 teaspoon hot paprika

12 ounces dark beer or ale

1 large clove garlic, minced or peeled

¼ cup chopped fresh cilantro plus additional for garnish

3 tablespoons fresh lime juice

¼ cup plus 2 tablespoons sour cream

Combine the beans and the water in a pressure cooker over high heat; bring to a boil. Cover, lock, and bring to high pressure over high heat. Reduce the heat to stabilize pressure and cook for 3 minutes.

Lower the pressure by the cold water–release method. Carefully remove the cover. Remove and drain the beans. Rinse out the cooker and return the beans to it. Add the tomatoes, onion, chile, ham, chili powder, cumin, oregano, paprika, and beer. Add minced garlic or press in a whole clove. Cover, lock, and bring back to high pressure over high heat. Reduce the heat to stabilize pressure and cook for 25 minutes.

Lower the pressure by the cold water–release method. Carefully remove the cover and stir in the cilantro and lime juice. Garnish each serving with 1 tablespoon of sour cream and a sprinkle of cilantro.

Appaloosa Bean Ragoût

Appaloosa beans bear striking black-and-white markings similar to those of the horse of the same name. Also known as cave beans, they supposedly originated in the Southwest near the ancient cave dwellings. Look for the sun-dried tomato paste in your supermarket's Italian section. We like to serve this dish with the Jalapeño Cornbread recipe that follows.

ELECTRIC
COMPATIBLE
with Revision:

Use the browning setting to bring the water and beans to a gentle boil. Lower the pressure using the quick-release button.

MAKES 4 SERVINGS

$1\frac{1}{4}$ cups dried appaloosa beans, picked over

3 cups water

2 small yellow onions, chopped (about $1\frac{1}{3}$ cups)

3 medium stalks celery, chopped (about 1 cup)

3 medium carrots, peeled and chopped (about 1 cup)

4 cloves garlic, chopped

2 tablespoons fresh oregano or 1 tablespoon dried oregano

1 tablespoon fresh thyme or $\frac{1}{2}$ tablespoon tried thyme

1 tablespoon cumin seeds

1 tablespoon sun-dried tomato paste

2 cups Smoked Turkey Stock (page 38), Turkey Stock (page 38), or defatted Chicken Stock (page 36 or canned)

$\frac{3}{4}$ teaspoon ground cumin

$\frac{1}{4}$ cup fresh lime juice

$\frac{1}{4}$ cup chopped fresh cilantro

1 jalapeño chile, cored, seeded, deveined, and chopped (about 1 tablespoon)

Combine the beans and the water in a pressure cooker. Bring to a boil over high heat. Cover, lock, and bring to high pressure over high heat. Reduce the heat to stabilize pressure and cook for 3 minutes.

Lower the pressure by the cold water–release method. Carefully remove the cover. Drain the beans and return them to the cooker. Add the onions, celery, carrots, garlic, oregano, thyme, cumin seeds, tomato paste, and stock. Cover, lock, and bring to high pressure over high heat. Reduce the heat to stabilize pressure and cook for 20 minutes.

Remove the pressure cooker from the heat and let the pressure drop naturally. Carefully remove the cover and stir in the ground cumin. Stir in the lime juice, cilantro, and jalapeño and serve.

Jalapeño Cornbread

If the asadero cheese, also called Chihuahua queso, is not available, substitute Monterey Jack cheese with chile peppers.

MAKES 4 TO 6 SERVINGS

1$\frac{1}{3}$ cups yellow cornmeal

$\frac{2}{3}$ cup all-purpose flour

1 tablespoon baking powder

1 teaspoon salt

$\frac{1}{8}$ teaspoon cayenne pepper

1 cup reduced-fat sour cream

$\frac{1}{2}$ cup buttermilk

1 large egg, well beaten

1 jalapeño chile, cored, seeded, deveined and chopped (about 1 tablespoon)

$\frac{1}{2}$ cup grated jalapeño asadero cheese

Preheat the oven to 425F (220C).

Sift the cornmeal, flour, baking powder, salt, and cayenne together into a small bowl.

Combine the sour cream and buttermilk in a large bowl. Whisk together, then whisk in the egg. Add the dry ingredients. Stir in the jalapeño and the cheese. Pour the mixture into a well-greased 9-inch-square baking pan. Bake for about 25 minutes, until the edges begin to brown.

Sauces, Chutneys, and Preserves

A 2-minute Cranberry Chutney that will put cranberry relish to shame next Thanksgiving? Robust Tomato Sauce fresh from scratch in 8 minutes? An old-fashioned Apricot Butter or Mincemeat just like Grandma used to make in 20 minutes?

No problem when you use your pressure cooker. Our sampling of sauces, preserves (do try such unique offerings as Tomato-Ginger Marmalade and Cranberry-Grapefruit Marmalade) can all be made in well under an hour from start to finish including all prepping of ingredients and precooking before bringing the cooker to pressure.

The sauces (including ragoûts), the Mincemeat, and the Cranberry Chutney should be stored in the refrigerator or frozen if they will not be eaten within two to three days. Green Apple Chutney and the preserves (including marmalades) should be hot-sealed in canning jars for home use, the filled jars put through a hot-water bath if you intend to ship them as gifts.

To hot-seal the jars, fill a large pot with enough water to cover by 1 or 2 inches over the top of the canning jars. Bring to a boil, carefully submerge the empty jars and their seals into the pot, and boil for about 5 minutes. Using tongs, remove a jar and fit it with a wide-mouthed canning funnel. Ladle in hot preserves to within about ¼ inch of the top

Processing Sauces, Chutneys, and Preserves

and wipe the mouth of the jar of any residue. Remove a cover and position it firmly atop the jar. Screw on a ring and place the jar upside down on a towel. (Fill each jar separately, so that neither the jar, the seal, nor the preserves will have a chance to cool.) Leave the filled jars upside down overnight, then check to see that the seals have taken (the covers should not pop when pressed).

To put the jars through a hot-water bath, fill a large pot with enough water to cover by at least 2 inches over the top of the filled canning jars. Fit the pot with a wire cooling rack that will raise the jars slightly off the bottom. Bring to a boil, carefully submerge the filled and sealed jars into the boiling water, and boil for about 15 minutes. When the jars have cooled sufficiently, check the covers to make sure that the seals have taken.

Meat Sauce

Our pressure cooker rendition of a classic bolognese, this sauce is ready in about 30 minutes—whereas bolognese usually simmers for hours. Thick and hearty, it tops pasta (especially penne, rigatoni, and other thick pasta) and polenta equally well and makes for a smashing lasagne. We call for canned tomatoes (use a good-quality Italian import), so you can enjoy this warming dish all winter long.

ELECTRIC
COMPATIBLE
with Revision:

Use the browning setting to initially cook the vegetables and then the meat.

MAKES ABOUT 9 CUPS

1 medium white onion, chopped (about 1 cup)

2 large stalks celery, finely chopped (about 1 cup)

2 large carrots, peeled and finely chopped (about 1 cup)

3 cloves garlic, chopped

$\frac{1}{2}$ tablespoon olive oil

1 pound ground beef sirloin

1 (28-ounce) can plus 1 ($14\frac{1}{2}$-ounce) can diced tomatoes

1 tablespoon dried rosemary

1 tablespoon fennel seeds

2 teaspoons dried oregano

$\frac{1}{2}$ teaspoon salt

$\frac{1}{4}$ teaspoon crushed red pepper flakes

Combine the onion, celery, carrots, garlic, and oil in a pressure cooker over medium heat. Cook, stirring occasionally, until the onion is translucent, 8 to 10 minutes. Mix in the beef and cook, stirring occasionally, until it is no longer pink and is crumbly, 4 to 5 minutes. Add the remaining ingredients. Cover, lock, and bring to high pressure over high heat. Reduce the heat to stabilize pressure and cook for 25 minutes.

Remove the pressure cooker from the heat and let the pressure drop naturally. Carefully remove the cover.

Store in the refrigerator 2 or 3 days or freeze up to 1 month.

Lamb Ragoût

An integral component of Cassoulet (page 163), this sauce is also good tossed with fettuccine or bucatini. We prefer lean lamb leg meat for this dish, but you could also use precut lamb stew meat, which usually comes from the shoulder.

MAKES 4 SERVINGS

1 large white onion, diced (about 1½ cups)

3 cloves garlic, minced

2 teaspoons olive oil

1 pound boneless lamb leg meat, trimmed and cut into ½-inch cubes

2 medium tomatoes, peeled, seeded, and diced (about 1½ cups) or 1 (14½-ounce) can diced tomatoes

½ cup dry white wine

1 teaspoon dried rosemary

½ teaspoon salt

⅛ teaspoon ground black pepper

Combine the onion, garlic, and oil in a pressure cooker over medium heat. Cook, stirring constantly, until the onion is translucent, about 4 minutes. Add the lamb and cook until it is no longer red and has browned lightly, 2 to 3 minutes. Stir in the remaining ingredients. Cover, lock, and bring to high pressure over high heat. Reduce the heat to stabilize pressure and cook for 15 minutes.

Remove the pressure cooker from the heat and let the pressure drop naturally. Carefully remove the cover.

Store in the refrigerator 2 or 3 days or freeze up to 1 month.

Tomato Sauce

Simple, straightforward, and unabashedly Italian, this all-purpose sauce is especially good in summer when fresh tomatoes are in season. When you chop them, save the juice to add to the pot. (We cut the tomatoes on a meat board with a built-in well.)

ELECTRIC
COMPATIBLE

MAKES ABOUT 5½ CUPS

6 medium tomatoes (about 3 pounds total), peeled, seeded, and chopped (about 5 cups)

1 medium yellow onion, diced (about 1 cup)

2 medium stalks celery, diced (about ¾ cup)

1 medium carrot, peeled and diced (about ½ cup)

2 cloves garlic, chopped

1 tablespoon dried basil

½ tablespoon dried oregano

¼ teaspoon crushed red pepper flakes

2 bay leaves

⅓ cup dry red wine

2 tablespoons tomato paste

Combine all the ingredients, except the tomato paste, in a pressure cooker. Cover, lock, and bring to high pressure over high heat. Reduce the heat to stabilize pressure and cook for 8 minutes.

Remove the pressure cooker from the heat and let the pressure drop naturally. Carefully remove the cover, discard the bay leaf, and transfer 1½ cups to a food processor or blender. Add the tomato paste and process until pureed; stir the mixture back into the sauce in the cooker.

Store in the refrigerator 2 or 3 days or freeze up to 1 month.

Cranberry Chutney

A perfect substitution for the ubiquitous cranberry relish, this will perk up your Thanksgiving buffet, at the height of cranberry season. The chutney will hold up well in the refrigerator for up to 5 days, so you don't have to wait until your holiday dinner preparation is at its most hectic pace.

MAKES ABOUT 4 CUPS

1 medium yellow onion, chopped (about 1 cup)

1 medium Granny Smith apple, peeled, cored, and chopped (about 1¼ cups)

1 (12-ounce) bag fresh cranberries

½ cup golden raisins

1½ tablespoons grated fresh ginger

1 cup firmly packed dark brown sugar

½ teaspoon ground cinnamon

¼ teaspoon ground cloves

½ cup cider vinegar

¼ cup fresh orange juice

¼ cup chopped walnuts

1 tablespoon grated orange zest

Combine the onion, apple, cranberries, raisins, ginger, brown sugar, cinnamon, cloves, vinegar, and orange juice in a pressure cooker. Stir to mix. Cover, lock, and bring to high pressure over high heat. Reduce the heat to stabilize pressure and cook for 2 minutes.

Remove the pressure cooker from the heat and let the pressure drop naturally. Carefully remove the cover and transfer the contents to a medium bowl. Stir in the walnuts and orange zest. Cover and refrigerate until the relish is thick and well chilled, about 4 hours.

Store in the refrigerator 5 days or freeze up to 1 month.

Green Apple Chutney

A smashing accompaniment to all sorts of grilled foods, this chutney also makes a delightful hors d'oeuvre spread on savory crackers over a thin layer of cream cheese. For a sweeter chutney, substitute very firm Fuji or Gala apples for the green Granny Smiths. If you can't find a McIntosh apple (which will fall apart easily as cooked and thicken the mixture), use a Jonagold.

ELECTRIC COMPATIBLE

MAKES ABOUT 6 CUPS

1 medium McIntosh apple, peeled, cored, and finely chopped (about 1¼ cups)

4 medium Granny Smith apples (about 2 pounds total), peeled, cored, and finely chopped (about 5¼ cups)

1½ cups golden raisins

1⅓ cups firmly packed dark brown sugar

2 tablespoons chopped crystallized ginger

2 teaspoons Curry Powder (page 32 or purchased)

½ tablespoon ground coriander

4 cloves garlic, minced

1 teaspoon salt

⅛ teaspoon cayenne pepper

2 teaspoons grated lemon zest

½ cup apple cider vinegar

Combine the apples, raisins, brown sugar, ginger, curry powder, coriander, garlic, salt, cayenne, lemon zest, and vinegar in a pressure cooker. Stir well to mix. Cover, lock, and bring to high pressure over high heat. Reduce the heat to stabilize pressure and cook for 4 minutes.

Remove the pressure cooker from the heat and let the pressure drop naturally. Carefully remove the cover. Whisk to break up the apples a bit more. Ladle into hot, sterile ½-pint or ¼-pint jars and seal immediately (see hot-sealing directions on page 175).

ELECTRIC
COMPATIBLE
with Revision:

*Compatible only if your
cooker works at low
pressure. Use the browning
setting to bring the mixture
to a gentle boil.*

Mincemeat

**This is a traditional mincemeat, replete with beef. When we can find
them, we like to add sour cherries to the mincemeat; use either fresh
cherries, frozen cherries that have been thawed, or canned and
drained sour cherries.**

MAKES ABOUT 10 CUPS; ENOUGH FOR 2 (10-INCH) PIES

1 small navel orange

8 ounces boneless beef chuck, finely chopped (about 1 cup)

8 ounces beef suet, finely chopped (about 1 cup, packed)

2 medium Granny Smith apples, peeled, cored, and diced
(about 3 cups)

1 medium Bartlett pear, peeled, cored, and diced (about 1¼ cups)

1 pound golden raisins (about 3 cups)

8 ounces currants (about 1 cup)

¾ cup mixed candied fruit and peel

1½ cups firmly packed dark brown sugar

½ cup dark molasses

½ cup brandy

8 ounces pitted sour cherries (about 1 cup) (optional)

3 ounces candied ginger in syrup, chopped (about ¼ cup) or
¾ teaspoon ground ginger

½ tablespoon ground cinnamon

½ tablespoon ground cloves

1 teaspoon ground nutmeg

½ teaspoon ground mace

Cut the orange into 8 pieces, removing the seeds but leaving the peel
intact, and finely chop it in a food processor (about ½ cup). Transfer
to a pressure cooker, along with the remaining ingredients. Bring to a
boil; cook, stirring occasionally, over medium heat, about 15 minutes.
Still over medium heat, cover, lock, and bring to low pressure. Adjust
the heat to stabilize pressure and cook for 20 minutes.

Lower the pressure by a quick-release method. Carefully remove the cover.

Store in the refrigerator 2 or 3 days or freeze up to 1 month.

MINCEMEAT PIES

Divide the mincemeat between 2 (10-inch) pie shells and top each with a second shell, crimping the edges together and making 3 steam vents in each with the tip of a sharp knife. Bake in a preheated 450F (230C) oven for 10 minutes, then reduce the heat to 350F (175C) and bake for about 20 minutes more, until golden.

Strawberry Preserves

Good old-fashioned strawberry preserves, served up just like you remember them! An added by-product of this recipe is the strawberry fluff you skim off at the end—when chilled, most kids and more than a few adults find the stuff irresistible spread on toast.

MAKES 4 CUPS

1 quart strawberries, hulled and sliced (about 5 cups)

3½ cups sugar

1 tablespoon Grand Marnier

Combine the strawberries, sugar, and liqueur in a large bowl and mix well. Set aside for about 30 minutes, until the sugar has dissolved. Mash with a potato masher.

Transfer the strawberry mixture to a pressure cooker. Cover, lock, and bring to high pressure over high heat. Reduce the heat to stabilize pressure and cook for 6 minutes.

Remove the pressure cooker from the heat and let the pressure drop naturally. Carefully remove the cover. Return the cooker to the

ELECTRIC
COMPATIBLE
with Revision:

Use the browning setting to bring the preserves to a boil (this will take a few minutes longer than over high heat on the stovetop). Before sealing in jars, make sure that a bit spooned onto an ice-cold plate coagulates into a spreadable mass.

stovetop. Bring the mixture to a rapid boil over high heat and boil until a bit spooned onto an ice-cold plate coagulates into a spreadable mass, 2 to 3 minutes. Skim off the fluff and ladle the preserves into hot, sterile ½-pint or ¼-pint jars and seal immediately (see hot-sealing directions on page 175).

ELECTRIC
COMPATIBLE
with Revision:

After pressure cooking, use the browning setting to bring the marmalade back to a boil. Before sealing in jars, make sure that a bit spooned onto an ice-cold plate coagulates into a spreadable mass.

Apricot-Orange Marmalade

We've done a number of preserve variations along the apricot-orange flavor spectrum, a favorite of ours; and we think this spectacular marmalade is heads above all previous versions. Heavenly spread on a scone or a toasted English muffin, Apricot-Orange Marmalade also makes a great glaze for poultry. You could also warm about ½ cup of it with ¼ cup chicken stock and 1 tablespoon port as a sauce for poultry.

MAKES 5 CUPS

2 large navel oranges

1 pound dried apricots, roughly chopped (about 2 cups)

3 cups sugar

2 tablespoons Grand Marnier

Cut each orange in half lengthwise, then slice thinly crosswise into half moons and remove the seeds. Combine in a large bowl with the apricots, sugar, and Grand Marnier. Stir well and set aside for about 1 hour, until the sugar has dissolved completely.

Transfer the mixture to a pressure cooker. Bring to a boil over high heat. Cover, lock, and bring to high pressure over high heat. Reduce the heat to stabilize pressure and cook for 5 minutes.

Remove the pressure cooker from the heat and let the pressure drop naturally. Carefully remove the cover. Return the cooker to the stovetop. Stirring constantly, bring the mixture back to a boil over high heat and boil until a bit spooned onto an ice-cold plate coagulates into a spreadable mass, about 1 minute. Ladle into hot, sterile ½-pint or ¼-pint jars and seal immediately (see hot-sealing directions on page 175).

Cranberry-Grapefruit Marmalade

Cranberry-Grapefruit Marmalade was the hit of the holiday season one year, showing up on crumpets, English muffins, and even toasted slices of rye bread. It has a refreshing hint of tartness—making it definitely an adult preserve. Don't worry if the marmalade appears a bit soupy when you first open the pressure cooker; it will harden to a perfect consistency as it cools.

 ELECTRIC COMPATIBLE

MAKES ABOUT 6 CUPS

2 medium ruby red grapefruit, unpeeled, each cut into 16 pieces and seeded

1 (12-ounce) bag fresh cranberries

4 cups sugar

¼ cup port

Roughly chop the grapefruit and cranberries in a food processor. Remove to a medium bowl. Add the sugar and port and set aside for about 20 minutes, until the sugar has dissolved and the mixture is soupy.

Transfer the grapefruit mixture to a pressure cooker and bring to a boil over high heat. Cover, lock, and bring to high pressure over high heat. Reduce the heat to stabilize pressure and cook for 6 minutes.

Remove the pressure cooker from the heat and let the pressure drop naturally. Carefully remove the cover. Ladle into hot, sterile ½-pint or ¼-pint jars and seal immediately (see hot-sealing directions on page 175).

Use the browning setting to bring the marmalade to a boil. Before sealing in jars, make sure that a bit spooned onto an ice-cold plate coagulates into a spreadable mass.

Tomato-Ginger Marmalade

A sophisticated and savory preserve, Tomato-Ginger Marmalade is every bit as good on a roast turkey sandwich as on a croissant. Use plum tomatoes so that you don't have to waste time and energy seeding them, as you would with larger tomatoes.

MAKES ABOUT 4 CUPS

2 pounds plum tomatoes (8 to 9 tomatoes), peeled and cut into chunks

1 navel orange (unpeeled), halved and thinly sliced

1 lemon (unpeeled), halved and thinly sliced

3 cups sugar

¼ cup chopped crystallized ginger

Combine the tomatoes, orange, lemon, and sugar in a large bowl. Mix and set aside until the sugar has dissolved and the mixture is soupy, about 10 minutes. Mix in the ginger.

Transfer to a pressure cooker and bring to a boil over high heat. Cover, lock, and bring to high pressure over high heat. Reduce the heat to stabilize pressure and cook for 14 minutes.

Remove the pressure cooker from the heat and let the pressure drop naturally. Carefully remove the cover. Return the cooker to the stovetop. Bring the mixture to a boil over high heat and boil until a bit spooned onto an ice-cold plate coagulates into a spreadable mass, 2 to 3 minutes. Ladle into hot, sterile ½-pint or ¼-pint jars and seal immediately (see hot-sealing directions on page 175).

Apricot Butter

We make the butter *and* put it through a hot-water bath in a single pressure cooker step in this recipe! Make sure that the canning jars are raised off of the bottom of the cooker a bit, placed on a trivet or a small wire rack. Although we like this butter, the intense flavor of which is derived from dried apricots, on the smooth side, you can also leave it flecked with bits of fruit if you prefer. Make sure that the rim of each jar is perfectly clean before sealing it or the seal may not take.

ELECTRIC
COMPATIBLE
with Revision:

Make the Apricot Butter in 2 batches.

MAKES ABOUT 5 CUPS

1½ pounds dried apricots, chopped (about 3 cups)

2 cups sugar

1 cup fresh orange juice

2 tablespoons light or golden rum

Combine the apricots, sugar, orange juice, and rum in a large bowl. Let sit at room temperature until the sugar has dissolved and the mixture is soupy, about 1 hour.

Scrape the mixture into a food processor and process until smooth. Ladle into sterilized ½-pint or ¼-pint jars. Wipe any residue off the jars with a damp cloth, place a sterile seal on top of each, and screw on the rings. Place a trivet or a small wire rack into a pressure cooker and the jars on the trivet. Add 6 cups water. Cover, lock, and bring to high pressure over high heat. Reduce the heat to stabilize pressure and cook for 20 minutes.

Remove the pressure cooker from the heat and let the pressure drop naturally. Carefully remove the cover.

Desserts

From Rum-Raisin Bread Pudding, which takes 17 minutes to prepare, to Sue B's Molasses-Cranberry Pudding or unique Persimmon Pudding, which take 40 minutes, the pressure cooker produces terrific steamed puddings—moist and more uniformly smooth and creamy than stovetop renditions, which tend to be crusty on the outside and soft inside. The Christmas Plum Pudding is spectacular; and even though one of our longest pressure cooking recipes at 90 minutes, it's considerably quicker in execution than the usual 4 hours or so.

And let's not forget Mango-Banana Crème Caramel (16 minutes), Coffee Flan (12 minutes), and individual Chocolate Pots de Crème (13 minutes), any of which could end the most elegant dinner party with a flourish. The menu also includes Apricot Cheesecake, which can be whipped up in 25 minutes, and Eggnog Cheesecake, which takes a little longer at 40 minutes. Do remember, however, in planning desserts that cheesecakes and custards are best served chilled and should therefore be made a few hours in advance.

Take care to wrap desserts securely in heavy-duty foil so that the water you add to the cooker will not penetrate the wrap. Place the mold or pan in the center of a sheet of foil that is about twice its size. Bring the long ends up over the top and crimp them together, then the short ends. Smooth the foil all around the sides tightly to the mold or pan.

Wrapping in Foil

Using a Trivet or Rack

Most pressure-cooked desserts need to be raised off the bottom of the cooker with a trivet or wire rack, just as you would place many into a hot-water bath were you going to oven-bake them. Make sure that there is about a 1-inch border all around between the dessert's mold or pan and the inside of the cooker to allow steam to circulate and the dessert to cook evenly. Most recipes call for lowering the pressure naturally and gently, just as you would let a cheesecake cool down in the oven.

Sue B's Steamed Molasses-Cranberry Pudding

We got this recipe from our buddy Deb Hendricks, who got it from Sue B in Canada, her guru and mentor in most things culinary. Sue B's original directions relied on visual doneness clues, but because peeking isn't permitted in our pressure cooker rendition, you'll just have to trust our timing. Deb says it is terrific, moister than the original, and also somewhat prettier and more regular in shape. Use a tall plum pudding mold if you have a large enough pressure cooker to accommodate it.

The tartness of the cranberries plays nicely off the heavy sweetness of the molasses. Leave it to clever Sue B to come up with the idea of freezing the cranberries (freeze at least 1 whole bag when they are in season, enough for two puddings), which will thaw while cooking but not explode as previously thawed cranberries might. If you're as athletic as Sue B, or just in the mood for an indulgence, consider the sinfully rich sauce that follows.

MAKES 12 TO 14 SERVINGS

> 1 tablespoon plus 1 teaspoon baking soda
>
> 1 cup dark molasses
>
> 1 cup boiling water, plus 3 cups room temperature water
>
> 3 cups all-purpose flour
>
> 2 tablespoons baking powder
>
> 2 cups fresh cranberries, frozen for at least 8 hours

Combine the baking soda, molasses, and boiling water in a large bowl. Stir well to blend. Stir in the flour and baking powder. Fold in the cranberries. Pour into a 6- to 8-cup mold and cover tightly with foil (see page 189). Place a trivet or a small wire rack into a pressure cooker, along with the room temperature water. Position the mold on the trivet. Cover, lock, and bring to high pressure over high heat. Reduce the heat to stabilize pressure and cook for 40 minutes.

Remove the pressure cooker from the heat and let the pressure drop naturally. Carefully remove the cover. Transfer the mold to a rack and let cool for 10 minutes before unmolding and serving.

ELECTRIC
COMPATIBLE
with Revision:

If your cooker is a model that can be set to cook for only 30 minutes, reprogram it for an additional 10 minutes after the pudding has cooked for 30 minutes.

Sue B's Sinful Hard Sauce

MAKES ABOUT 2 CUPS

2 cups heavy cream

1 cup sugar

1 cup unsalted butter

Combine the cream, sugar, and butter in a medium saucepan over medium-high heat. Bring to a boil, reduce the heat to low, and simmer for 15 minutes, taking care not to let the mixture boil over.

ELECTRIC
COMPATIBLE

*Too large for a 4- or
5-quart pressure cooker.*

Persimmon Pudding

This exceedingly moist pudding derives its distinctive flavor from sweet-tart persimmons, available in the fall and winter months. Whether you use the short, flat American variety (most of which come from Indiana) or the teardrop-shaped Japanese persimmons, be sure to select soft, very ripe persimmons because persimmons, which start out incredibly tart, become sweeter as they ripen. Make the pudding in a mold with a tightly fitting cover or wrap it tightly in foil.

MAKES 12 TO 14 SERVINGS

2 cups all-purpose flour

1 tablespoon baking powder

1 teaspoon baking soda

2 teaspoons ground cinnamon

$^3/_4$ teaspoon salt

$^1/_2$ teaspoon ground ginger

4 large eggs

2 cups firmly packed dark brown sugar

3 (6-ounce) persimmons, peeled and mashed (about 2 cups)

5 tablespoons unsalted butter, melted

¼ cup Grand Marnier

1 tablespoon pure vanilla extract

½ cup golden raisins

½ cup chopped walnuts

3 cups water

Mix together the flour, baking powder, baking soda, cinnamon, salt, and ginger in a medium bowl.

Combine the eggs and brown sugar in a large bowl. Beat with an electric mixer at medium speed until the mixture is thick and frothy, about 2 minutes. Beat in the persimmons, butter, Grand Marnier, and vanilla. Add the flour mixture and beat just to combine. Fold in the raisins and the walnuts. Pour the batter into an 8-cup mold that has been coated with cooking spray.

Put a trivet or small wire rack into a pressure cooker, along with the water. Cover the mold tightly with foil (see page 189) and place it on the trivet. Cover the pressure cooker, lock, and bring to high pressure over high heat. Reduce the heat to stabilize pressure and cook for 40 minutes.

Remove the pressure cooker from the heat and let the pressure drop naturally. Carefully remove the cover. Remove and uncover the mold. Let the pudding cool for 10 minutes in the mold on a rack, then unmold it onto the rack and cool to room temperature.

Plum Pudding

We make this favorite old-fashioned Christmas dessert, chock-full of dried fruit, in the traditional tall plum pudding mold with a center column (to produce a ring) and a tight-fitting cover. The mold, however, is tall enough that it will fit only in our 8-quart capacity pressure cooker. If you use another type of mold to accommodate a smaller cooker, wrap the pudding tightly in foil as directed on page 189. For a

ELECTRIC
COMPATIBLE

Too large for a 4- or 5-quart pressure cooker.

luscious gift with a bit of added flavor, wrap the unmolded pudding in a large piece of cheesecloth that has been soaked in rum.

MAKES 12 TO 14 SERVINGS

1 pound mixed dried fruit

8 ounces dried figs

8 ounces pitted dried dates

4 ounces seedless raisins

4 ounces golden raisins

4 ounces currants

4 ounces dried cranberries

¾ cup golden rum

4 ounces beef suet, finely chopped (about ½ cup)

4 large eggs

1 cup firmly packed dark brown sugar

1 tablespoon plus 1 teaspoon chopped crystallized ginger

2 teaspoons grated orange zest

2 teaspoons ground cinnamon

1 teaspoon ground nutmeg

½ teaspoon salt

2 cups plain breadcrumbs

1 cup all-purpose flour

½ tablespoon baking powder

Chop the mixed dried fruit, the figs, and the dates. Combine with the raisins, currants, and dried cranberries in a large bowl. (You should have about 8 cups.) Mix in the rum and set aside to soak for about 1 hour.

In another bowl, combine the suet, eggs, brown sugar, ginger, orange zest, cinnamon, nutmeg, and salt. Add the mixture to the dried fruit and mix well. In a third bowl, combine the breadcrumbs, flour, and baking powder. Add the dry ingredients to the fruit mixture and mix thoroughly. Scrape the very thick batter into an 8-cup mold that has been coated with cooking spray, pushing down to pack the mold firmly.

Put a trivet or a small wire rack into a pressure cooker, along with the water. Cover the mold tightly with the lid or foil and place it on the trivet. Cover the pressure cooker, lock, and bring to high pressure over high heat. Reduce the heat to stabilize pressure and cook for 90 minutes.

Remove the pressure cooker from the heat and let the pressure drop naturally. Carefully remove the cover. Remove and uncover the mold. Let the pudding cool for 15 minutes in the mold on a rack, then unmold it onto the rack and cool to room temperature.

White Chocolate Cherry Rice Pudding

ELECTRIC
COMPATIBLE

We prefer this decadently rich and creamy dessert warm, but it could also be served chilled. Use Arborio rice or another short-grained rice, such as Carnaroli. Dried cherries, once a pricey gourmet shop exclusive, are now stocked by many supermarkets. Substitute dried cranberries or raisins if you like. We've found through trial and error that cherry liqueur boosts the taste of the dried cherries over the edge—we prefer the subtle contrasting accent lent by raspberry-flavored Chambord or orange-flavored Grand Marnier.

MAKES 6 SERVINGS

1 cup Arborio rice

1 cup heavy cream

1 1/3 cups water

1/2 cup dried cherries

1/2 tablespoon pure vanilla extract

1 large egg, beaten

1/2 cup white chocolate chips

1 tablespoon Chambord or Grand Marnier

Combine the rice, cream, water, cherries, vanilla, and egg in a pressure cooker. Stir to mix, cover, lock, and bring to low pressure over medium heat. Adjust the heat to stabilize pressure and cook for 8 minutes.

Lower the pressure by a quick-release method. Carefully remove the cover. Stir in the white chocolate and Chambord or Grand Marnier. Serve about ¾ cup per person.

Rum-Raisin Bread Pudding

Newly rediscovered bread puddings seem to be getting trendier in their ingredient combinations by the day, but we prefer such homey, old-fashioned renditions as rum raisin. For a special treat if you have been very good, slice the chilled pudding, broil the slices until lightly browned and serve with Sue B's Sinful Hard Sauce (page 192).

ELECTRIC
COMPATIBLE
with Revision:

Lower the pressure using the quick-release button.

MAKES 8 SERVINGS

8 ounces French bread (about ½ loaf), cut into 1-inch cubes (about 6 cups)

2 cups nonfat half-and-half

2 large eggs

2 tablespoons dark rum

¾ cup sugar

1 teaspoon ground cinnamon

1 cup golden raisins

4 cups water

Combine the bread cubes and the half-and-half in a large bowl. Stir and set aside for about 20 minutes. In a small bowl, whisk together the eggs, rum, sugar, and cinnamon. Pour the mixture over the bread cubes and stir in the raisins. Transfer to a greased 7-inch springform pan and wrap securely with foil (see page 189).

Place a trivet or a small wire rack into a pressure cooker and the wrapped springform pan onto the trivet. Add the water. Cover, lock, and bring to high pressure over high heat. Reduce the heat to stabilize pressure and cook for 17 minutes.

Remove the pressure cooker from the heat and let the pressure drop naturally. Carefully remove the cover. Gently remove the spring-form pan from the cooker and unwrap the pudding. Refrigerate for at least 4 hours before unmolding and serving.

VARIATIONS

Replace the rum with 2 tablespoons Amaretto and add ⅓ cup sliced almonds along with the raisins.

Replace the rum with 3 tablespoons Marsala and the raisins with ¾ cup chopped mixed candied fruit and peel.

Replace the rum with 3 tablespoons pure maple syrup and replace the golden raisins with ½ cup seedless raisins and ½ cup chopped walnuts.

Baked Apples

This dessert goes especially well with the Apple Pork Loin (page 76) and can actually be prepared simultaneously in the pressure cooker; place the wrapped apples on both sides of the loin and omit the additional water. Although we're partial to the taste combination of finishing a meal that features pork with these apples, they could be cooked with and served after virtually any compatible main course that is pressure cooked for about the same length of time.

MAKES 4 SERVINGS

¼ cup golden raisins

¼ cup chopped walnuts

2 teaspoons chopped crystallized ginger

¼ cup firmly packed light brown sugar

2 tablespoons brandy

4 medium Gala apples, cored

4 teaspoons apricot preserves

1 cup water

Mix together the raisins, walnuts, ginger, brown sugar, and brandy in a small bowl.

Place each apple in the center of a 12-inch square of double-thickness foil. Pack the cavity of each with a generous 2 tablespoons of the raisin mixture and top with 1 teaspoon of the preserves. Gather the foil up around the apples and twist closed.

Put a trivet or a small wire rack into a pressure cooker, along with the water. Place the apples on the trivet. Cover, lock, and bring to high pressure over high heat. Reduce the heat to stabilize pressure and cook for 15 minutes.

Remove the pressure cooker from the heat and let the pressure drop naturally. Carefully remove the cover. Remove the apples and let cool to room temperature before gently unwrapping them, spooning some of the excess juices trapped in the foil wrappers over each serving.

Eggnog Cheesecake

For last year's Christmas Eve dinner on the Outer Banks, always a special occasion, we came up with this dense New York–style cheesecake (which didn't make it through much of the holidays because it was the target of numerous midnight refrigerator raids). Don't worry if the cake cracks across the top in the pressure cooker because you will be frosting it anyway. To carry out the eggnog theme, sprinkle some freshly grated nutmeg over the top.

ELECTRIC
COMPATIBLE
with Revision:

If your cooker is a model that can be set to cook for only 30 minutes, reprogram it for an additional 10 minutes after the cake has cooked for 30 minutes.

MAKES 8 SERVINGS

CHEESECAKE

3 (8-ounce) packages cream cheese, at room temperature

$^3/_4$ cup sugar

$^1/_3$ cup eggnog

3 large eggs

1$^1/_2$ tablespoons brandy

3 tablespoons all-purpose flour

2 cups water

TOPPING

$^1/_2$ cup sour cream

1 tablespoon sugar

$^1/_4$ teaspoon brandy

$^1/_4$ teaspoon ground nutmeg

Put the cream cheese into a large bowl. Beat with an electric mixer at high speed just enough to soften, 30 to 45 seconds. Mix in the sugar. Beat in the eggnog, then the eggs, 1 at a time. Reduce the speed to low and beat in the brandy and flour.

Scrape the mixture into a greased 7-inch springform pan and wrap the pan tightly in foil (see page 189). Place a trivet or a small wire rack into a pressure cooker, along with the water. Position the springform pan on the trivet. Cover, lock, and bring to high pressure over high heat. Reduce the heat to stabilize pressure and cook for 40 minutes.

Remove the pressure cooker from the heat and let the pressure drop naturally. Carefully remove the cover. Gently remove the spring-form pan from the cooker and unwrap the cheesecake. Cool to room temperature in the pan on a rack.

Meanwhile, make the topping. Combine the sour cream, sugar, brandy, and nutmeg in a small bowl. Mix until blended. Spread the topping over the cheesecake and chill for at least 3 hours in the refrigerator before serving.

Apricot Cheesecake

ELECTRIC COMPATIBLE

No time, no fuss, no hot water bath needed when you make cheese-cake in a pressure cooker! Just make sure the springform pan is tightly wrapped in foil before placing it into the cooker and let the cheesecake cool to room temperature before releasing the spring. This simple, straightforward cake (a cheesy rather than a cakey cheese-cake) is moist thanks to the wet heat of the pressure cooker. It will freeze nicely for up to 3 months. Substitute lower-fat and -calorie cream cheese, if desired, but please do not use gummy nonfat cream cheese.

MAKES 8 SERVINGS

4 (8-ounce) packages cream cheese, at room temperature

1 cup sugar

4 large eggs

2 tablespoons all-purpose flour

$^1/_3$ cup heavy cream

$^1/_2$ tablespoon pure vanilla extract

8 ounces dried apricots, chopped (about 1 cup)

$2^1/_2$ cups water

With an electric mixer at medium speed, cream the cream cheese in a large bowl. Add the sugar and mix until well blended. Beat in the eggs,

1 at a time. Reduce the speed to low and beat in the flour, cream, and vanilla. Stir in the apricots. Pour the mixture into a greased 7-inch springform pan.

Put a trivet or a small wire rack into a pressure cooker, along with the 2½ cups water. Wrap the springform pan tightly with foil (see page 189) and place it on the trivet. Cover, lock, and bring to high pressure over high heat. Reduce the heat to stabilize pressure and cook for 25 minutes.

Remove the pressure cooker from the heat and let the pressure drop naturally. Carefully remove the cover. Remove and gently unwrap the springform pan. Let the cheesecake cool to room temperature on a rack, then chill in the refrigerator for at least 4 hours before serving.

VARIATION

Strawberry Cheesecake: For variety, try Strawberry Cheesecake in lieu of Apricot Cheesecake. Omit the apricots and melt about 3 tablespoons currant jelly in a small saucepan or a microwave oven. Paint the chilled cheesecake with melted jelly, top with 2 pints hulled strawberries, and drizzle with some more jelly.

ELECTRIC
COMPATIBLE
with Revision:

*Lower the pressure using
the quick-release button.*

Coffee Flan

You could also make this intriguing custard in two 3-cup molds and pressure cook it in batches or cut the ingredients in half for a single small mold. Substitute 1 cup nonfat liquid egg substitute for the eggs if you're watching fat and rum, Amaretto, or Frangelico for the coffee liqueur as strikes your fancy of the moment.

MAKES 12 SERVINGS

2 (12-ounce cans) evaporated skim milk

1 (14-ounce) can nonfat sweetened condensed milk

4 large eggs

⅓ cup coffee liqueur (see below or purchased)

1 cup sugar

2¼ cups water

Combine the evaporated milk, sweetened condensed milk, eggs, and liqueur in a large bowl. Whisk until well blended.

Combine the sugar and ¼ cup of the water in a small, heavy saucepan. Cook, stirring constantly, over high heat until the sugar has dissolved, 1 to 2 minutes. Reduce the heat to medium and cook, occasionally swirling the pan, until the mixture is a deep caramel color, 7 to 10 minutes.

Pour the caramel mixture into a 6-cup mold, swirling to coat the bottom and partway up the sides of the mold. Pour in the milk and egg mixture. Put a trivet or a small wire rack into a pressure cooker, along with the remaining 2 cups water. Wrap the filled mold tightly with foil (see page 189) and place it on the trivet. Cover, lock, and bring to high pressure over high heat. Reduce the heat to stabilize pressure and cook for 12 minutes.

Remove the pressure cooker from the heat and let the pressure drop naturally. Carefully remove the cover. Transfer the mold to a rack and cool to room temperature, then chill for at least 4 hours in the refrigerator before serving.

Homemade Coffee Liqueur

**If you like pricey coffee liqueur as much as we do, in recipes
and on the side, you may be tempted to whip up a batch of your own,
which will have a shelf life of 2 to 3 months.**

MAKES ABOUT 2 1/2 CUPS

1 cup ground full-bodied coffee beans

1 1/2 cups boiling water

3/4 cup granulated sugar

1/4 cup firmly packed light brown sugar

1/2 teaspoon pure vanilla extract

1 1/2 cups vodka

Mix together the ground coffee and boiling water. Allow to steep
for 2 minutes. Fit a sieve with a coffee filter and strain the coffee into
a medium saucepan over low heat. Add the sugars and cook, stirring
constantly, just until steaming, about 5 minutes, taking care not to
bring to a boil. Remove from the heat and allow to cool. Stir in the
vanilla and vodka. Set aside for 3 to 4 days before serving.

ELECTRIC
COMPATIBLE

Chocolate Pots de Crème

These chocolate egg custards, somewhat denser than flan, are a heavenly holiday indulgence. Even nonchocoholic Kevin, whose taste runs more to nutty concoctions, loves them. Use tall, thin ramekins, more of which will fit into your pressure cooker than squatter ramekins; classic pots de crème have covers, others should be tightly wrapped in foil.

MAKES 4 SERVINGS

1¼ cups milk

¾ cup heavy cream

4 ounces bittersweet chocolate, broken up

2 tablespoons sugar

6 large egg yolks, lightly beaten

2 tablespoons rum

2 cups water

Combine the milk and cream in a medium saucepan over medium heat. Scald just until bubbles begin to form around the edge, 3 to 4 minutes. Remove the pan from the heat and whisk in the chocolate and sugar, continuing to whisk until the chocolate has melted. Cool to room temperature, then whisk in the egg yolks and rum. Pour ¾ cup of the mixture into each of four (1-cup) pots de crème or 1-cup ovenproof ramekins and cover each tightly with a lid or foil (see page 189).

Put a trivet or a small wire rack into a pressure cooker, along with the water. Place the ramekins on the trivet. Cover, lock, and bring to high pressure over high heat. Reduce the heat to stabilize pressure and cook for 13 minutes.

Remove the pressure cooker from the heat and let the pressure drop naturally. Carefully remove the cover. Transfer the ramekins to a rack to cool. Serve at room temperature or refrigerate until well chilled before serving.

Mango-Banana Crème Caramel

Nonfat sweetened condensed milk lends this refreshing custard an ethereal quality, less rich and dense than our Coffee Flan (page 202), which is made with evaporated skim milk. It's the perfect finish to a decadent holiday meal. Dotted with bits of mango pulp, the custard has a slightly granular texture that we find interesting. If you prefer a smoother consistency, strain the mixture before molding. You could easily substitute 1 cup nonfat liquid egg substitute for the eggs if desired.

ELECTRIC
COMPATIBLE
with Revision:

Lower the pressure using the quick-release button.

MAKES 12 SERVINGS

4 large eggs

1 (14-ounce) can nonfat sweetened condensed milk

1 1/2 cups skim milk

1/4 cup golden rum

1 large banana, mashed (about 1/2 cup)

1 medium mango, peeled, pitted, and finely chopped (about 1 1/2 cups)

1/2 cup sugar

2 tablespoons plus 2 cups water

Combine the eggs, milks, rum, banana, and mango in a large bowl. Whisk until the custard mixture is frothy.

Combine the sugar and 2 tablespoons of the water in a small, heavy saucepan. Cook, stirring constantly, over high heat until the sugar has dissolved, 1 to 2 minutes. Reduce the heat to medium-low. Cook, periodically swirling the pan, until the caramel is a deep, rich color, 7 to 10 minutes.

Pour the caramel mixture into a 6-cup mold, swirling to coat the bottom and part way up the side. Add the egg mixture to the mold. Put a trivet or small wire rack into a pressure cooker, along with the remaining 2 cups water. Wrap the mold tightly with foil (see page 189) and place it on the trivet. Cover, lock, and bring to high pressure over high heat. Reduce the heat to stabilize pressure and cook for 16 minutes.

Remove the pressure cooker from the heat and let the pressure drop naturally. Carefully remove the cover. Let the mold cool to room temperature on a rack. Chill for at least 3 hours in the refrigerator before serving.

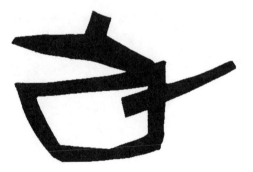

SOURCE

Contact the following manufacturers for information on their pressure cookers.

Fagor
800-207-0806

Kuhn Rikon
800-662-5882
Web site: www.kuhnrikon.com

Magefesa
888-787-9991
Web site: www.magefesausa.com

Meal 'N Minutes
800-557-9463

Mirro
800-518-6245
Web site: www.mirro.com

Presto
800-877-0441
Web site: www.gopresto.com

Salton
800-423-0336
Web site: www.salton-maxim.com

T-Fal
800-395-8325
Web site: www.t-fal.com

INDEX